100 HOTELS
OF A LIFETIME

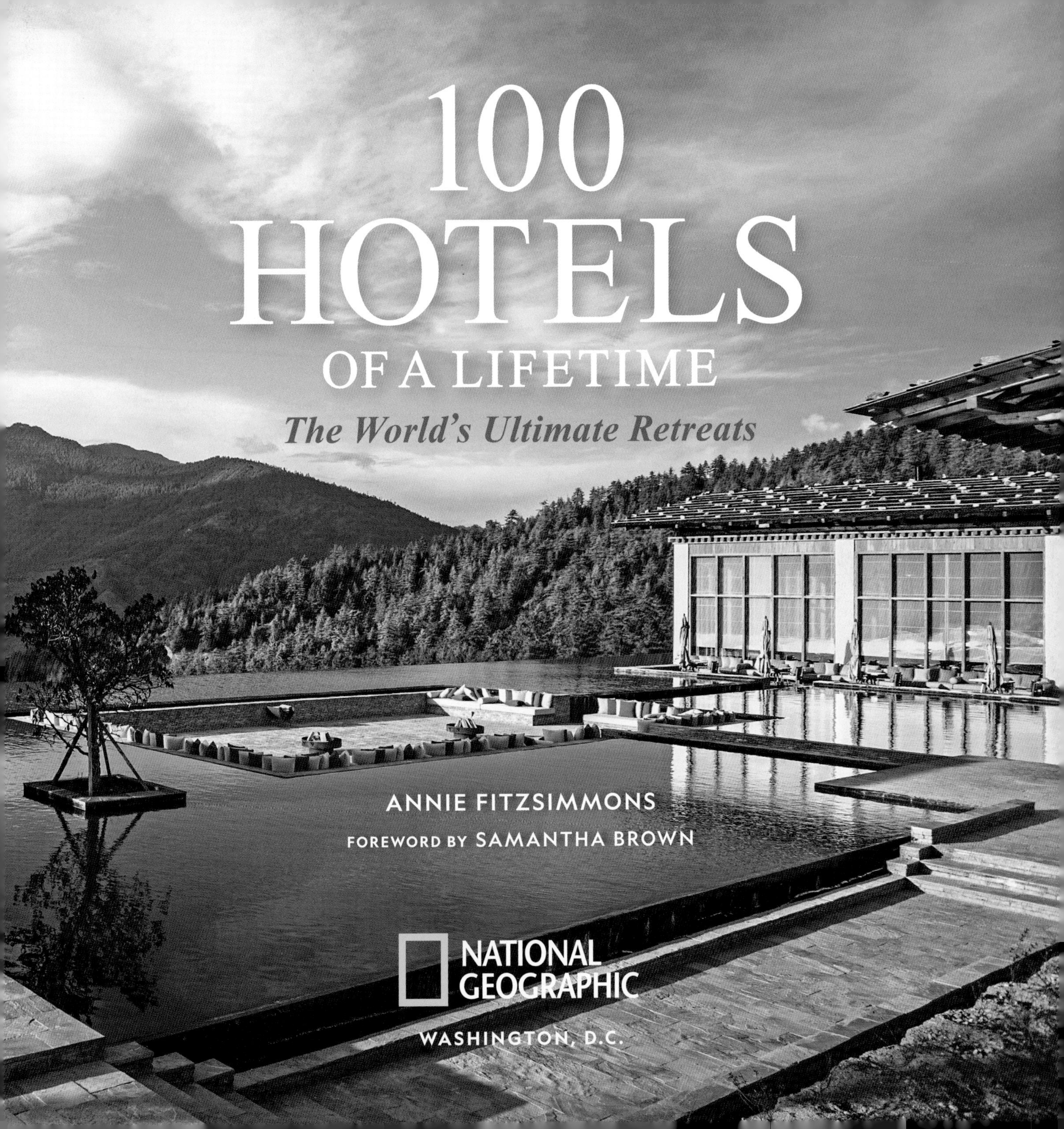

100 HOTELS OF A LIFETIME

The World's Ultimate Retreats

ANNIE FITZSIMMONS

FOREWORD BY SAMANTHA BROWN

NATIONAL GEOGRAPHIC

WASHINGTON, D.C.

CONTENTS

OPPOSITE: A guest draws a bath in her lavish suite at Zarafa Camp in Botswana (page 348).

PAGES 2-3: The Prayer Pavilion at Six Senses Thimphu (page 301) is one of the lodge's defining features; it is set adjacent to the reflecting ponds and offers a view of the valley.

FOREWORD

I first met Annie more than 13 years ago at a café in Brooklyn, New York. She was writing an article about my career, but we so quickly fell into a comfortable conversation that our roles as interviewer and interviewee dissolved. On that very day, a great and lasting friendship was firmly established—one that began with a shared love of travel that has shaped our careers and evolved into so much more. Our friendship is a relationship that has always felt comfortable and celebratory at the same time.

That dichotomy is what I respect so much about Annie's work as a travel writer and now as an author. She has the exceptional ability to celebrate what makes travel unique and deliver it in a way that feels comfortable to all, demonstrating that no matter how luxurious and exclusive an experience is, each of us can enjoy and connect to it.

For instance, I'm reading an early version of *100 Hotels of a Lifetime* on a cold February day on a break from teaching my 11-year-old twins, who no longer have snow days but instead must log in to remote school with a full list of classroom assignments that I must facilitate. In between teaching, I open the book and am immediately transported to the Amalfi Coast in Italy. I can almost feel the Mediterranean sun on my face, as if I'm sitting on the terrace of Borgo Santandrea (page 30), a hotel that appears to be carved into a cliffside and offers sea views for days. I can practically hear the surf below as I'm about to take a sip of my perfectly frothed cappuccino before I'm interrupted by a child who needs help multiplying fractions.

What Annie conveys so well is a hotel's ability to allow you to be someone else, somewhere else. With 20 years of writing experience under her belt, she understands that a deep-rooted connection to a destination is a hotel's ultimate amenity.

There are surprising choices throughout this book, too. While Annie connects us to the grand hotels we've long admired (Claridge's in London,

ABOVE: **Treat yourself to a gourmet picnic on the beach at Baros Maldives (page 302).**

page 54; the Beverly Hills Hotel in Los Angeles, California, page 164; and Raffles Singapore, page 280), she also highlights hotels that are without a doubt hidden gems. Some of these places are, against all odds in today's hospitality business, still family owned (Grand Hotel Tremezzo in Italy, page 22; also on the stunning cover of this beautiful volume). Many feel like a totally new discovery. For instance, though I've been a professional traveler for 25 years, I had never heard of Ascona, Switzerland. Now I must find my way to this small town on Lake Maggiore to enjoy the colorful and eccentric experience of Hotel Eden Roc Ascona (page 86), which was designed by an Ascona native.

What I believe readers will love most about *100 Hotels of a Lifetime* is

ABOVE: Mont Cervin Palace in Zermatt, Switzerland (page 88), offers tons of family-friendly activities indoors and out.

OPPOSITE: A giraffe joins a trio of guests for lunch at Sirikoi Lodge in Kenya (page 324).

how the book has a choose-your-own-adventure appeal. There's no need to read in order; just decide where you want to travel to for the next 15 minutes or several hours. Once my job as elementary school teacher is done for the day, I plan to make a hot cup of tea and open the book to enjoy hotels in Scotland.

Tomorrow, I plan on being a guest somewhere in Africa.

—Samantha Brown
Host and executive producer of Emmy Award–winning
Samantha Brown's Places to Love

INTRODUCTION

When I told people I was writing a book about the world's best hotels, the first question was, "Do you need an assistant?" Sometimes, it was a demand: "Take me with you!"

I started on this book during one of the COVID-19 lockdowns. I was living in London, unable to go anywhere at all. I missed so much of my work, which has taken me all over the globe for two decades, many as National Geographic's first and only Urban Insider reporting on cities, culture, hotels, restaurants, and creative and passionate people around the world. I missed the invigorating sense of being in a great hotel, a magic, comfortable base to explore a destination and connect to people both outside and in the hotel—smartly dressed bartenders, hotel managers, and housekeepers (who are heroes).

As the lockdown went from weeks to months—and then came again—all I wanted was to leave my home. One thing that I never say about a great hotel is that it "feels like home." (Ett Hem in Stockholm, page 78, is an exception.) I want a hotel to feel *better* than my home, with no piles of laundry on a random chair or dishes in a sink. The best hotels in the world take you out of daily routines and allow you to access different parts of your personality. I was craving that escapism.

The other question I got while writing and researching this book: "How do you choose which hotels make the cut?"

It wasn't easy, but I considered several factors: Ultimately, the hotel had to feel completely and absolutely of the destination—these couldn't be hotels you could find anywhere else in the world. Hotels of a lifetime offer immersion into a destination. They are the equivalents of great tour guides who are friendly and helpful but nudge you to go farther and explore more.

I had to be cognizant of geographical and brand diversity (quite honestly, the entire book could have been about great hotels in Italy). And yes, all Four

ABOVE: **The Fife Arms' Victoriana Suites (page 66), decorated with vintage antiques and artwork, showcase the hotel's history as a 19th-century Scottish coaching inn.**

PAGES 12–13: **In the winter wonderland of Bavaria, Schloss Elmau (page 114) has its own ice rink for guests.**

Seasons, Belmond, and Oetker Collection hotels are usually flawless. But I also wanted to make some surprising choices—a boutique hotel in Berlin, a collection of properties in Norway, a castle in Slovenia, a moderately priced hotel in Ortygia, Sicily—my home base for a glorious weeklong food tour.

Choosing hotels that welcomed anyone inside—even if they are not staying the night—was extremely important to me. Have a drink or dinner, book afternoon tea, go to the hotel spa. I included a few exceptions, such as the all-inclusive Castle Hot Springs (page 194). And it's not possible to pop into some of them, such as The Brando in French Polynesia (page 374) or a safari lodge in Africa, just for a drink. But I understand many of these hotels are expensive, and I want everyone, staying guest or not, to be able to experience them. (My tip: I always recommend checking for lower rates in the low or shoulder seasons.) And I hope, through these pages, to also take you there from your armchair.

Through my work, I have always been determined to showcase the immense value and power of luxury travel from a new perspective. Luxury hotels support and sustain communities in immeasurable ways. As reported by International Luxury Travel Market, the $2.05 trillion ecosystem supports about 170 million jobs, 90 percent of which are family or small businesses.

The industry is a leader in following the U.N.'s three pillars of sustainability: economic, social, and environmental. And what starts at a higher level often trickles down to the overall travel industry. I highlight many of these efforts throughout the book.

The late Keith Bellows, *National Geographic Traveler* editor in chief and a mentor, taught us to frame sustainability as "preserving the places we love the most." National Geographic's original mission statement promised to "illuminate and protect the wonder of our world." The best hotels do both, while setting the scene for unforgettable memories through hospitality.

But no matter the nightly rate or top-tier service, the greatest luxury is time spent enjoying these hotels and the destinations they inhabit, connecting with people we love or reconnecting with ourselves. I have been lucky to see Venice several times now and no longer feel the need to see every church and monument, but instead want to linger on a hotel terrace on a sunny day, soaking up the Venetian air.

ABOVE: **After a day of skiing in Aspen, refuel with a hearty feast at Hotel Jerome's J-Bar (page 186).**

OPPOSITE: **Visit Relais Christine's Spa Guerlain (page 94) for a Parisian spa treatment.**

I spent 20 years building a career in travel writing, visiting many of the world's greatest hotels for both work and pleasure. Through two decades, I gained an understanding of the brands and how they have evolved, and I have formed some strong opinions about hotels. (Please, a simple light switch is fine, one that doesn't need a manual.)

An astute mathematician may count the hotels in this book and realize that more than 100 have been included. Making this selection was challenging—I could have included myriad hotels—and so some hotels that are often booked together as an experience count as one entry, such as the Old Cataract in Aswan and Winter Palace in Luxor, Egypt (page 316), and the Six Senses properties in Bhutan (page 298). I also added Bonus Stays for additional ideas.

I'm just trying to go for volume two. Who wouldn't, with this job?

PART ONE

EUROPE

Manicured greenery and an award-winning golf course surround Adare Manor, a five-star hotel in County Limerick, Ireland (page 150).

VENICE, ITALY

HOTEL CIPRIANI

One of Italy's most iconic hotels is known for its distinct location and top-of-the-line service.

YEAR ESTABLISHED: **1958** NUMBER OF ROOMS: **96** FAMOUS FEATURE: **Swimming pool**
WHEN TO GO: **April–June or September–October**

If forced to choose only one hotel of a lifetime, the crown jewel just might be the Belmond Hotel Cipriani, set on Giudecca Island, a seven-minute boat ride from Venice's St. Mark's Square. The hotel is as much a part of Venice as the canals and palaces, fish market, flooding, and crowds.

Giuseppe Cipriani, founder of Venice's legendary Harry's Bar, had already invented the Bellini cocktail when he decided to build a hotel here, partly financed by members of the Guinness family. Though considered a bit foolish at the time, Hotel Cipriani's island location—which feels worlds apart—helps make it the most relaxing hotel in Venice today, allowing guests a reprieve from the busier establishments along the canals.

Also relaxing? The Olympic-size seawater swimming pool, a rarity in Venice. Built 13 years after the hotel opened, it is still one of the main draws of the property. Some of the most requested rooms have a private terrace and direct access to the pool.

A perfect day in the hotel starts with a leisurely buffet breakfast enjoyed at lagoon-view tables, followed by sightseeing. To help combat the effects of overtourism, the hotel offers special private programs, like a tour of Venetian fashion through museum storage rooms, and slow travel options, like cycling on (almost) uninhabited islands or visiting lagoon wineries.

Return for the *aperitivo* (appetizer) hour at Bar Gabbiano. The hotel's grounds and gardens are fragrant with fresh flowers and herbs like sage, basil, thyme, and marjoram, which are put to good use in cocktails. One of the most

BOOK IT NOW

Make reservations early and keep timing in mind: The hotel closes for a few months in the winter, usually beginning in mid-October.

OPPOSITE: The luxe Palladio Suite at Hotel Cipriani includes a plush king-size bed and 180-degree views of the Venetian Lagoon.

PAGES 20-21: The luxurious Hotel Cipriani sits perched on the edge of an island in the Venetian Lagoon.

beloved bartenders in the world is charming and precise Walter Bolzonella, who recently retired from Bar Gabbiano after 43 years. George Clooney wrote the foreword to Bolzonella's book, *Cocktails in Venice: Tales of a Barman,* which you can buy on-site. The most requested cocktail at the bar is the original Bellini, the same recipe the hotel's founder created in 1948.

Have dinner at high-end Cip's Club with a view of the Doge's Palace and St. Mark's Square. If you eat at a trattoria in Venice, like Antiche Carampane or Osteria Ca' d'Oro alla Vedova, speed back to your bed at the Cipriani on one of the world's most romantic (and quickest) boat rides under the stars.

If you don't stay overnight at the hotel, you can still book a table for lunch or dinner and find your way to the hotel by boat from St. Mark's Square.

In the midst of overtourism and the threat of rising canal waters, Hotel Cipriani remains—and will always be—an exceptional haven.

DRINK IT UP

Until you can enjoy it at Bar Gabbiano, try the Cipriani's classic Bellini at home with this recipe: Pour two ounces (6 cL) white peach puree (you can purchase this in local specialty shops or online) into a chilled flute, then fill it the rest of the way with four ounces (12 cL) very cold Prosecco DOCG Brut. Stir gently with a spoon. A light layer of foam will naturally form at the top.

LAKE COMO, ITALY

GRAND HOTEL TREMEZZO

A destination for jet-setters past and present, this hotel delivers on its luxurious reputation.

YEAR ESTABLISHED: **1910** NUMBER OF ROOMS: **84** FAMOUS FEATURE: **Lake Como views**
WHEN TO GO: **April–May and September–October**

The arrival to the Grand Hotel Tremezzo on Lake Como is cinematic. The first view: an art nouveau facade that has become synonymous with Wes Anderson whimsy, though it was built long before the movie director was born. The second view sits opposite the hotel: the floating swimming pool, seemingly suspended in the lake, with the pink-and-yellow village of Bellagio (very different from its Vegas namesake) in the distance.

The next thing you'll notice is bright and fizzy orange, the signature color here. There are orange awnings, orange deck chairs, and orange-and-white-striped pool umbrellas. Inside, pops of orange are equally everywhere, down to the leather remote control case in every room and the custom-scented bottles of Aqua Como toiletries.

The hotel's interiors are sophisticated and bold, with rich reds and golds in the main lobby and vibrant green, purple, pink, and orange seating in the bar. Rooftop suites have views to Bellagio and whirlpool tubs and include Suite Greta, which pays homage to Greta Garbo. The actress called the hotel "that happy, sunny place" in the 1932 Oscar-winning film *Grand Hotel*.

"The Grand Hotel Tremezzo is one of those hotels that always remains in your heart," says Andrea Grisdale, founder of IC Bellagio. "The incredible

LOCAL ACCESS

"A favorite escape of mine is Osteria da LuCa in Cernobbio," says Andrea Grisdale. "I love to have Sunday morning breakfast—a cappuccino and brioche—there, then enjoy a gorgeous walk in the heart of nature before returning to enjoy *aperitivo* time with a glass of local wine and local cheeses, salumi, and homemade breads."

OPPOSITE: Tour the scenic waters of Lake Como aboard a rental motorboat.

PAGES 24-25: Vacation like a movie star during a stay at the elegant Suite Greta, an ode to the renowned actress Greta Garbo.

passion that the owners have put into the property oozes everywhere you go."

Anyone who has met Valentina De Santis agrees: An encounter with her feels downright life-changing. You feel so lucky to be in the soulful, passionate, and funny presence of one of the hardest-working and most beloved hoteliers in the business. Her family has owned the property since 1975—her mother's father bought it originally, and she grew up in the hotel. Ask for the torta Valentina if it's not listed on the menu.

Though the lake views are central to the hotel experience, the back gardens are worth climbing to see a new wooden statue of De Santis's childhood bear, Bobo. (An adorable stuffed Bobo, with an orange ribbon, is given to every child that visits the resort.) The seven acres (2.8 ha) of gardens were designed by Emilio Trabella, a renowned botanist and landscaper who was known in Lake Como as the "prince of gardens" and as a "plant whisperer" by his friend and collaborator, architect Renzo Piano. George Clooney might agree;

EAT IT UP

"With the most extensive views of the lake, my favorite place to eat is the Trattoria Baita Belvedere in the hills above Bellagio," says Andrea Grisdale, founder of IC Bellagio, who has lived near Bellagio for decades. "This tiny family-run trattoria makes the best polenta with braised beef that I have ever tasted. Their wine list is impressive, with many local wines from the Valtellina region. My favorite table in the cooler months is the table for two in front of the fireplace."

GRAND HOTEL
TREMEZZO
PALACE
PALACE

ABOVE: **After a day exploring the lake, eat a rich meal at Grand Hotel Tremezzo.**

OPPOSITE: **On the shores of Lake Como, find Grand Hotel Tremezzo's impressive facade and floating swimming pool.**

Trabella also worked on the gardens at his Lake Como home. At the top of the property's hill is a centuries-old olive tree. Back down in the hotel grounds, watch out for the 150-year-old strawberry tree near the T Shop.

Spa lovers will appreciate the T Spa, housed in the historic Villa Emilia and completely redone in 2016 with an indoor infinity pool and hammam-style suite.

Though all the dining options (ranging from casual to fine dining) are flawless, many guests have a soft spot for the wood-fired pizzas turned out by the garden pool. T Bar is another good option. Start with an *aperitivo* and relax as you decide if you'll have dinner here or move over to the restaurant.

PORTOFINO, ITALY

SPLENDIDO, A BELMOND HOTEL

Stay for the celebrity treatment at a grand hotel that's more than a century old.

YEAR ESTABLISHED: **1902** NUMBER OF ROOMS: **70** FAMOUS FEATURE: **Coastal views** WHEN TO GO: **March–October**

Welcome to Italy's grande dame of coastal hotels. Here, it is much less about what you can accomplish in the destination, but rather about simply existing in one of the most spectacularly beautiful hotels—with equally spectacular views!—in the world.

Splendido, A Belmond Hotel, Portofino, a beautiful hotel nestled in the region that gifted pesto to the world, is set just outside the chic village of Portofino, between Genoa and the over-discovered Cinque Terre in Liguria. It is easy to settle into the glamour and history of this former 16th-century monastery turned hotel. The hotel first opened in 1902, but became a favorite of the jet-set elite in the 1950s and '60s. Clark Gable, Ava Gardner, and Humphrey Bogart count among its celebrity guests, as does, more recently, Beyoncé. This is where Richard Burton famously proposed to Elizabeth Taylor on the terrace of one of the largest suites. (And even if you aren't a staying guest, you can order the pomodoro pasta dish "Homage to Elizabeth Taylor" at the hotel's La Terrazza.) The actress returned many times.

And it's no wonder why: Nearly all of the rooms face the water, and other highlights include breakfast on the hotel's terrace overlooking the picture-perfect Portofino harbor; an on-property *gelateria* (ice-cream shop); beautiful terraced gardens; a Dior Spa; and a saltwater infinity pool overlooking the coast. Though a honeymoon favorite, it also has a fantastic kids' club (ages four to 12) for those looking for a family-friendly stay.

ALTERNATE STAY

Portofino is just five minutes away, with a 14-room sister hotel, Splendido Mare, that reopened in 2021 but evokes the look and feel of the 1950s, one of the seaside village's golden eras.

OPPOSITE: Enjoy dining with a view of the sparkling Ligurian Sea at Splendido.

AMALFI COAST, ITALY

BORGO SANTANDREA

This relative newcomer has already made its mark on the hotel scene.

YEAR ESTABLISHED: **2022** NUMBER OF ROOMS: **29** FAMOUS FEATURE: **Breakfast on the terrace**
WHEN TO GO: **May or September**

It is not an easy feat to create a new icon on the Amalfi Coast, which for decades has been lined with some of the very best hotels on the planet, all surrounded by fragrant lemon and other citrus trees. But only a few years after opening, Borgo Santandrea has cemented itself in the cliff-side coastal hall of fame.

In the tiny fishing village of Conca dei Marini and overlooking Sophia Loren's former villa on one side, the hotel was born from the roots of two families in the hospitality business on the island of Ischia, where they still operate a few properties. It embodies the Italian good life, as well as the owners' passion for artwork and furniture, much of which is sourced from personal collections.

The hotel's design, first and foremost, might be called a ceramic fairy tale, inspired by Gio Ponti's first hotel in Sorrento, the famous Parco dei Principi. With an Amalfi Spritz in hand, you could spend hours looking at the tiles in 39 patterns evoking the deep and varied blues of the landscape, all hand-painted on handmade terra-cotta.

The mid-century furniture—think deep-blue velvet sofas and clean lines—is a fresh and elegant departure from typical Amalfi Coast style. At the on-site beach club, which accesses a private white pebbled beach—an extremely rare luxury for the coast—you can enjoy sun lounging and Italian tapas, such as deep-fried spaghetti and mini pizzas. Eight elevators built into the cliffs whisk

CLOSE BY

In 1962, First Lady Jacqueline Kennedy visited the Amalfi Coast. She stayed in nearby Ravello but visited Conca dei Marini for waterskiing, to see friends, and to eat at La Tonnarella. Today, the classic Italian beach restaurant still serves Kennedy's favorite dish—Lo Spaghetto di Jacqueline, made with zucchini, pancetta, and Parmesan.

OPPOSITE: Stay in a premium suite at Borgo Santandrea, with an infinity pool and sea view.

PAGES 32–33: The sun sets over Conca dei Marini, a small maritime town on the Amalfi Coast.

you to the hotel's various levels, but for those able and willing, the vertical walk up and down through 200-year-old giant blueberry trees, potted lemon trees, olive trees, and a centuries-old arch that was once the gate to the city of Amalfi is absolutely heavenly. The spa pays homage to the owners' homeland with a treatment using Ischia mud, enhanced with thermal mineral water and salts.

The breakfast experience is so unique that it is tempting to keep it a surprise. First, it is served until noon, allowing for hours of lingering on the terrace with endless Mediterranean views. You are invited into the kitchen, as if you were visiting an old friend, to peruse and choose from a mouth-watering breakfast buffet. Among the choices: slices of airy, fruit-studded panettone (yes, an Italian Christmas specialty—but why not year-round?), pans of roasted vegetables paired with freshly made eggs, fruit and vegetable juices, and dozens of pastries and cakes. The coffee, as per usual in Italy, is exquisite.

Try to see the hotel from a boat, where it looks like an impossible feat of engineering.

QUOTABLE

"One of the newest gems on the Amalfi Coast, this exquisite property has breathtaking views of the Mediterranean and offers a rare private beach. The breakfast experience at this hotel is truly unparalleled and I would say worthy of a Michelin star. From the meticulously hand-painted tiles that adorn the floors to the flowers planted across the property, this hotel exudes an aura of serenity." —Susan Zurbin-Hothersall, New York–based travel adviser

TUSCANY, ITALY

BORGO SAN FELICE

History and charm combine for an authentic stay in a former Tuscan village.

YEAR ESTABLISHED: **1992** NUMBER OF ROOMS: **60** FAMOUS FEATURE: **Wine tasting**
WHEN TO GO: **April–May or September–October**

You will see the word "borgo" all over Italy; its meaning is simple—"village." Where you see "borgo," there is, or was, a village. Borgo San Felice is built into protected buildings of the eighth-century village of San Felice, located 20 minutes from Siena in the heart of the Chianti wine region. Everything here centers around the beautiful Piazza San Felice, now heart of a soulful Tuscan property, which makes its own top-quality wine.

The historic buildings have been converted into beautiful rooms and suites. Plus, the former oil mill (Il Frantoio) has been transformed into the hotel's spa. Of two churches on the property, one dates back to A.D. 714.

Long walking paths, quiet spots for picnics, and pots of lemons tell you you're in Tuscany—this is a postcard countryside stay. "There is 100 percent a sense of place starting with the arrival up the driveway lined with cypress trees and a backdrop of the Tuscan hills," says Andrea Grisdale, founder of IC Bellagio. "Having a Michelin-starred restaurant and a trattoria on-site while being surrounded by vineyards makes it so hard to leave."

The hotel is also known for its award-winning sustainability measures. The hotel boasts a zero-waste certification, runs on 100 percent renewable energy, sources foods like chocolate and coffee from sustainable and ethical sources, and champions social farming projects. It also employs young people with disabilities or difficult backgrounds through a long-running program.

OPPOSITE: The picturesque Borgo San Felice, including its old chapel, piazza, and pool

FLORENCE, ITALY

THE PLACE FIRENZE

This contemporary gem provides unique access to oft crowded tourist destinations.

YEAR ESTABLISHED: **2003** NUMBER OF ROOMS: **20** FAMOUS FEATURE: **Curated experiences**
WHEN TO GO: **Year-round**

Renaissance glory meets *la bella vita* on the terrace at THE PLACE Firenze, a 20-room boutique hotel set on the Piazza Santa Maria Novella in Florence. Guests can sip a Shakerato (an Italian-style shaken iced coffee) while overlooking Leon Battista Alberti's masterpiece basilica (completed in 1470). In fact, the letters etched on the facade of the church inspired the custom font created for the hotel. Some of the rooms have views of the basilica, and all are stylish and contemporary, with linen sheets and elegant finishings.

In a city where you often fight through crowds, the key word here is "access." Led by beloved longtime general manager Claudio Meli, who boasts the ultimate book of insider contacts to Florence, guests can access the Place of Wonders, a curated offering of uncommon experiences that help preserve Florentine tradition. Choose from visits to a violin maker, a historic paper factory, or the nearby Museo Marino Marini, a contemporary art museum with a breathtaking hidden treasure—Alberti's Rucellai Chapel, a scale model of the Church of the Holy Sepulchre in Jerusalem (said to be the tomb of Jesus of Nazareth).

THE PLACE evokes the spirit of Florence across centuries. Even if you're not a staying guest, you should book a table for breakfast on the terrace, sip coffee from a colorful Ginori 1735 porcelain cup, and enjoy the view.

OPPOSITE: Gaze across at the medieval Santa Maria Novella church while dining alfresco at The Kitchen & The Bar.

ROME, ITALY

HOTEL DE RUSSIE

Have yourself a Roman holiday in a luxurious hotel steps away from prime attractions.

YEAR ESTABLISHED: **1901** NUMBER OF ROOMS: **120** FAMOUS FEATURE: **The Shakerato**
WHEN TO GO: **Shoulder season (January–February)**

It is hard to claim a better location in Rome than the Hotel de Russie, located on Via del Babuino, a short walk from the Spanish Steps (but seemingly a world away from the chaos). The hotel and gardens—now part-owned by Sir Rocco Forte as part of his small hotel group—were designed in the early 1800s by the same architect who modernized the buzzy Piazza del Popolo.

On a hot day in Rome, there is no better respite than Le Jardin de Russie, the hotel's lush, terraced garden and restaurant, and a relaxing urban meeting spot that anyone can book for lunch or dinner. Here, you can also enjoy the bar's sublime version of an Italian Shakerato—a smooth and frothy iced coffee—rattled with gusto in a cocktail shaker by expert bartenders. (Ask for it unsweetened; it's that good.)

Pablo Picasso is said to have stayed at the hotel for several months in 1917 and often leaned out his window to pick oranges. Those citrus trees still fill the garden with scent and color today. And the colorful, bold Picasso Suite, with a wraparound terrace, pays homage to the artist. One of the dreamiest of the hotel's 34 suites has a long, south-facing terrace that overlooks the narrow Via Margutta, which makes for a gorgeous sunset view of the city's rosy rooftops.

Rome may feel overwhelming with its crowds, so try visiting in January or February, when the weather is cool but not freezing and great for walking. "Offseason" in Rome feels absolutely perfect—and you'll find lighter crowds.

CLOSE UP

Watching Gregory Peck and Audrey Hepburn zoom around Rome on a Vespa in *Roman Holiday* (1953) will never get old. The final scene, in which Hepburn gives a farewell speech as a princess, was filmed in the jaw-dropping Sala Grande at Palazzo Colonna, a 15-minute walk from Hotel de Russie. Sala Grande is open to visitors on Saturday mornings only. Though the movie may be in black-and-white, the in-person interiors are dazzling.

OPPOSITE: Order a cocktail or wade in the saltwater hydropool at De Russie Spa.

ORTYGIA, ITALY

HOTEL GUTKOWSKI ORTYGIA

In a less visited part of Sicily, this quaint hotel shines in setting and charm.

YEAR ESTABLISHED: **1999** NUMBER OF ROOMS: **26** FAMOUS FEATURE: **Foodie finds**
WHEN TO GO: **April–June or October**

This small, locally run hotel overlooks the Ionian Sea from one of the most beautiful small cities in all of Italy: Ortygia. You'll see lots of cacti and leafy greenery lining the streets; twinkly lights and iron terraces marking thoroughfares; and one of the most strikingly beautiful cathedrals and piazzas in all of Italy.

Ortygia itself is a masterpiece and maze of baroque architecture. Everything on the island is within a 15- to 20-minute walk, and you'll find Hotel Gutkowsi set just a bit off the town's main center. The hotel feels wonderfully homespun, with a second-floor terrace—a great place for an *aperitivo*—overlooking the water. Breakfast is not huge but is filled with market finds like berries, cheese, and eggs; the excellent restaurant, Gutkowskino, is also fueled by local produce.

Sicily is attracting more travelers and hotel investors thanks to *White Lotus* (season two), which features the Four Seasons San Domenico Palace in Taormina. But it feels like a gift to discover this lesser known part of Sicily while staying in an intimate and delightful hotel.

OPPOSITE: Spend a peaceful evening watching the sunset from a Hotel Gutkowski balcony.

PAGES 42–43: Built in the 13th century on Ortygia, Castello Maniace juts dramatically out into the Mediterranean Sea.

A base in Ortygia is a smart choice. Just a short drive off the island via a small bridge to Syracuse brings you to Sicily's interior landscape, filled with thousands of citrus and olive trees, and other charming towns like Noto and Ragusa, where you can peel back the layers of what makes this region a food dynamo.

Many Sicilian farmers practice biodynamic agriculture. They eat ricotta and almonds a thousand different ways and drizzle local olive oil on everything, all paired with a glass of wine from the Etna vineyards. Wine expert and author Benjamin Spencer calls it a "boutique terroir," stemming from the "10,000-foot lava lasagna" that is the simmering fury of Mount Etna. But the most iconic Sicilian snack, often eaten for breakfast on hot days, is soft brioche with gelato or granita inside.

MEET UP

Rome-based author Elizabeth Minchilli runs small group tours focused on food culture in lesser traveled areas of Italy, including Sicily, Puglia, and Parma. Her daughter, Sophie, also runs small food tours in Rome. On her Sicily tour, Minchilli brought attention to the charm of this hotel, which offers a window into the authentic farming and food culture with visits to organic olive oil and almond farms and vineyards.

COUNTY MAYO, IRELAND

ASHFORD CASTLE

History, beauty, and hospitality come together in this tried-and-true favorite.

YEAR ESTABLISHED: 1939 **NUMBER OF ROOMS:** 83 **FAMOUS FEATURE:** Falconry
WHEN TO GO: May–June

Of all the beautiful hotels on the Emerald Isle, Ashford Castle reigns supreme with extra luck of the Irish. It evokes the history, beauty, and hospitality of the country like no other. Here, you stay in a real, genuine castle, but with every comfort of a luxury hotel, including the latest technology, state-of-the art facilities, delicious food and wine, and only-in-Ireland experiences.

Located in County Mayo, less than an hour from Galway, the original castle dates back to 1228, but much of what we see today was created by Irish royalty of a different ilk: the famed Guinness brewing family, who bought Ashford Castle in the mid-1800s. Today, it is owned by a legendary hotelier family, the Tollmans, who poured a deep passion for design—and the necessary money—into a restoration project that showcases Irish talent and brands like Magee and Waterford Crystal.

The 800-plus-year-old stones—and therefore, bones—of the castle are intact, but the work that has been done on the interiors is jaw-dropping. The deepest shades of emerald, ruby, and gold decorate the common areas and guest rooms. Roaring fires in cozy wood-paneled rooms are a luxurious contrast to the bucolic 350 acres (142 ha) of grounds to explore. On those grounds is the esteemed Ireland's School of Falconry, where guests can take lessons. It's an experience that allows you to connect with the beautiful hawks and their unique personalities—and, if you're lucky, with newborn baby hawks, known as eyases.

Compared to the historic castle, the spa and fitness suite is relatively new,

AFTER CHECK-IN

A visit to Joyce Country Sheepdogs, a family-run farm 30 minutes from Ashford Castle, is not to be missed. Surrounded by unspoiled Irish countryside, you'll learn from charming locals about the culture of sheep farming and living in this part of the world and discover the unique personalities of sheepdogs and what drives them.

OPPOSITE: Consume specialty tea and homemade pastries during afternoon tea in Ashford Castle's Connaught Room.

PAGES 46–47: Situated in the oldest wing of Ashford Castle, the Reagan Presidential Suite has an antique four-poster bed and expansive views of Lough Corrib.

set in a greenhouse-style extension with a small relaxation pool that serves as a welcome retreat when the rain inevitably comes.

The most beautiful rooms are situated in the castle and offer views of Lough Corrib. Not one room or suite feels like home—unless your home style veers to maximalist royal castle vibes—which is what you want staying at a place like this. Ashford Castle is a window into another world and time, offered through exquisite design: The walls are lined with mahogany and artwork, silk drapery, four-poster beds, and views that confirm you are most definitely in Ireland.

The nearby village of Cong has long attracted fans of *The Quiet Man,* a beautiful travelogue for the west of Ireland starring John Wayne and Maureen O'Hara. They filmed at the castle in 1951, and relics of the movie can be seen throughout the area. But you don't have to be a fan to love the quaint cottages and cute cafés of Cong, a 15-minute walk from the castle. If you haven't seen the movie, it's regularly shown in the on-site cinema, outfitted with 32 cozy red velvet chairs.

DRINK IT UP

Book afternoon tea with wonderful views in the Connaught Room for an Ashford tradition since 1868. You can roll straight into drinks at the Prince of Wales Bar, built in the late 1800s and later named for King George V (grandfather to Queen Elizabeth II), who visited here when he was the Prince of Wales in 1905.

ABOVE: A child poses with a hawk at Ireland's School of Falconry at Ashford Castle.

OPPOSITE: Located in the lush Irish countryside, the idyllic castle boasts 350 acres (142 ha) of grounds for visitors to explore.

With such luxurious surroundings, it is a testament to the staff that you feel cocooned in comfort and never once intimidated by the regal digs at Ashford Castle. (Also, the luxury is very apparent once you taste the quality of the desserts: Ashford has a full-time director of chocolate and patisserie.) Many members of the team have worked at Ashford for decades. You may also be greeted by the hotel's resident Irish wolfhounds in the Oak Hall, a nod to the playful nature of the hotel.

At this ultimate Irish retreat, the Gaelic phrase *céad míle fáilte* (one hundred thousand welcomes) echoes through the halls. It's no wonder so many guests return again and again.

LONDON, ENGLAND, U.K.

THE MILESTONE HOTEL & RESIDENCES

A friendly staff and top-notch design make this hotel stand out from the London crowd.

YEAR ESTABLISHED: **1922** NUMBER OF ROOMS: **62** FAMOUS FEATURE: **Residences with kitchens**
WHEN TO GO: **Year-round**

As in New York City and Paris, choosing one hotel of a lifetime in London is nearly impossible. There are the grande dames—the Connaught, Claridge's (page 54), the Savoy, and the Mandarin Oriental Hyde Park. And there are new icons: the Corinthia, the Peninsula London, and more.

But the Milestone Hotel & Residences seems both unequivocally British (charming, polite, unobtrusive) *and* under the radar enough that it still feels like a hidden gem you want to keep all to yourself.

Located across from Kensington Palace, the Milestone has royal tales to tell, but is too discreet to share them (also very British). Walk out to High Street Kensington for shopping, up into Notting Hill, or to the museums of South Kensington. The location is, in a word, unbeatable.

The best suites (there are 13 of them) overlook Kensington Gardens. The crown jewel is the golden and emerald green Hermès Suite, which is anchored by a bronze four-poster bed, art deco furnishings, and vintage Hermès scarves framed on the walls. Another showstopper is the Noel Coward Suite, with wall-to-wall leopard print.

OPPOSITE: Mirrored double doors invite guests into a marble bathroom in the Noel Coward Suite.

PAGES 52–53: The Milestone's equestrian-inspired Stables Bar pays homage to the original use of the building.

For families, the killer appeal of the Milestone lies in the six residences. Cook in your own kitchen after grabbing groceries from High Street Kensington (or Waitrose for the sophisticated Brit's favorite mainstream option), or order room service from the hotel—the best of both worlds. All rooms are dog- and cat-friendly, still rare for any hotel.

Adults can enjoy a signature Old-Fashioned while lounging in a green leather banquette at the Stables Bar, a small space lined with horse paintings. Or grab a drink to go and peruse the light-filled Conservatory.

The Milestone is part of the family-owned Red Carnation group (along with Ashford Castle, page 44). That familial vibe matters: Thanks to the longevity of the staff, this hotel stands out among its London peers for its top-notch hospitality. Longtime general manager Andrew Pike is one of the best in the business, as are the top-hatted, smiling greeters at the door and the concierge team.

ALTERNATE STAY

Part of the excellent Doyle Collection, the Marylebone is set in a charming urban village on Marylebone Lane, minutes from High Street. Visit the Wallace Collection, a free museum with a collection of 15th- to 18th-century art on display. A highlight is the Venetian Room, filled with paintings of Venice originally created for British tourists who had visited the city on their Grand Tour.

LONDON, ENGLAND, U.K.

CLARIDGE'S

One of the most loved and most storied properties in the world, this quintessential London hotel continues to set new standards.

YEAR ESTABLISHED: 1856 NUMBER OF ROOMS: 269 FAMOUS FEATURE: High tea WHEN TO GO: Year-round

There is nowhere in the world like the art deco lobby at Claridge's. Enter through the hotel's revolving door and you may ask yourself, Is this the center of the world? It certainly feels like it as you glide across the black-and-white checkered marble floor, surrounded by guests just as likely to be European royalty as they are a "regular Joe" here to celebrate a birthday at the world-famous afternoon tea. All are welcomed here with exceptional hospitality.

Claridge's opened in 1856, after a stint as a guesthouse. Soon after, guests included Queen Victoria, Prince Albert, and almost all major royals and celebrities to modern day. The main spaces in the hotel have remained the same since its 1929 art deco transformation.

Most recently, Claridge's has debuted a subterranean urban spa. (The hotel stayed open during construction; workers used their hands and shovels—no power tools—to dig five stories beneath Mayfair so as not to disturb the guests above.) It also offers two newer, showstopping suites: the Residence and the four-bedroom Penthouse, which has one of the best views in London and evokes the feeling of sailing a yacht in the sky. Rooms are exquisite and varied, thanks to a diverse set of designers hired to work on different rooms and decor components.

Two oft told stories speak to the essence of Claridge's: Once, a diplomat called the hotel just before the wedding of Princess Elizabeth to Philip in 1947. He asked to speak to "the king"; the telephone operator responded: "Certainly, sir, but which one?"

AFTER CHECK-IN

All of central London is within walking distance of Claridge's. You can be in Soho or Marylebone quickly, or go to Liberty or Selfridges to shop. But right across from the hotel is South Molton Street, a diagonal, twinkly-lit, pedestrianized shopping street—one of London's prettiest—with jewelry, clothing, and coffee shops, all set in Georgian-era buildings.

OPPOSITE: A spread of sweet and savory treats is served at Claridge's Champagne Afternoon Tea.

PAGES 56–57: The Grand Piano Suite, designed by Diane von Furstenberg, showcases her refined style and signature velvet and silk touches.

Master Artisans
ANDO

Another time, American actor Spencer Tracy famously remarked that he'd rather go to Claridge's than heaven when he died.

Yet, with such a storied history, the hotel continues to evolve and keep things exceedingly cool. For instance, the much anticipated Christmas tree in the lobby brings the crème de la crème to Claridge's every year. Among the designers? Louis Vuitton, Christian Dior, Jimmy Choo, and Alexander McQueen.

All of London awaits exploration outside, but it's very easy to cocoon yourself in Claridge's and never leave. Afternoon tea is not only central to life at Claridge's but also one of the city's time-honored traditions. It's a bucket-list experience that's ideally booked months in advance. Tea is served on striped porcelain dishes in the hotel's signature shade of jade green.

The Foyer (where tea is served) is the center of hotel life, with a fantastical Dale Chihuly sculpture hanging above extraordinarily fresh flower bouquets. The hotel also has a 1930s-style bar, the

ALTERNATE STAY

The Connaught, a sister property to Claridge's, is another of Mayfair's best hotels. It feels like it's from an earlier British era with its dark-paneled wood, a six-story mahogany staircase that Ralph Lauren loved so much he replicated it in his New York flagship store, and a bar consistently voted one of the best in the world. Visit the pink-hued Connaught Patisserie to see—or order—pastries and treats that could double as works of art.

Fumoir, plus Claridge's Bar, the Painter's Room cocktail bar, and a high-ceilinged main restaurant. The most recent addition, ArtSpace Café, offers coffee and pastries and a rotating art gallery beneath.

Everything is completely glamorous here, but children are also very welcome. On arrival, they receive a mini Claridge's suitcase, a personalized teddy bear with a top hat, sweets, and more.

Even if you can't stay the night, come through the famous revolving doors for tea or a drink, to order the famous chicken pie, or to gawk at the Christmas tree come holiday season. Claridge's is a legend for a reason, and you'll feel lucky to be here.

ABOVE: Step outside Claridge's and explore the beautiful district of Mayfair.

OPPOSITE: Healing and relaxation await visitors to the renowned Claridge's Spa.

VARIOUS LOCATIONS, ENGLAND, U.K.

THE PIG HOTELS

Across England, find a game-changing collection of boutique country hotels.

YEAR ESTABLISHED: **2011 (the original PIG)** NUMBER OF ROOMS: **12–32 (varies by property)**
FAMOUS FEATURE: **The 25-Mile Menu** WHEN TO GO: **Year-round**

Many properties evoke that classic English countryside experience: Chewton Glen with its tree houses and cooking school; the Newt in Somerset, set on a working farm; Babington House in the rolling Cotswolds; Coworth Park near Ascot in Berkshire; Heckfield Place with its incredible dining program. Finding the perfect country retreat depends on how far you want to travel, how much you want to spend, and how much grandeur you want with your rolling landscape views.

But in the category of comfortable luxury without eye-watering prices sits THE PIG brand, a game changer for the English countryside experience. As the chain says straight up: "We don't do formal."

Today, there are 11 PIG hotels throughout England, each centered around its own kitchen garden.

The first PIG hotel made its debut deep in the New Forest of Hampshire in 2011. The choice of location was idyllic: The scenery is so magical here that it would be unsurprising to find little English countryside fairies sprinkling pixie dust on the thatched roofs and country pubs. The owners wanted to create a laid-back, but still chic, brand with a more reasonable price point than those at the inns and hotels in the surrounding area. And they succeeded, in part thanks to their now famous walled kitchen garden that sprung an innovative concept: the "25-Mile Menu," found at all 11 properties.

Staying at a PIG is like touring England through delicious, hyperlocal food sources. Everything made and served at each hotel is sourced from the kitchen garden or from within a short distance of the restaurant.

AFTER CHECK-IN: CORNWALL

From THE PIG in Cornwall, visit nearby Padstow to dine at the restaurants and explore the shops of Rick Stein, one of England's most celebrated chefs and TV hosts. It all started when Stein opened the Seafood Restaurant here in 1975.

OPPOSITE: Curl up by the cozy fireplace in this seating area at THE PIG at Combe.

PAGES 62-63: At THE PIG near Bath, Big Comfy Luxe rooms offer a plush four-poster bed and a claw-foot tub.

Every PIG menu has a cheeky vibe, a taste of typical British humor. Choose from starters like garden bits, piggy bits, and fishy bits, or "A Selection of Plant-Based Dishes, Mostly Picked This Morning."

Make it a goal to hit all the "PIGs in the litter," or pick a favorite:

THE PIG at Brockenhurst, New Forest, Hampshire: Stay at the original PIG for the fairy-tale Hampshire vibes and the walled kitchen garden that started it all.

THE PIG in the wall, historic Southampton: If you're catching a cruise from Southampton on the *Queen Mary 2,* this is where you want to stay the night before you embark. The only PIG in a city is set within the medieval city walls.

THE PIG near Bath, Somerset: This is a charming country base to visit the Roman baths and Georgian architecture of Bath, a 20-minute drive away.

THE PIG on the beach, Dorset: This version of THE PIG is set within the Jurassic Coast, a 95-mile-long (153 km) UNESCO World Heritage site known for incredible fossil finds, a stunning coastline, and beaches.

AFTER CHECK-IN: HAMPSHIRE

For those traveling with kids, pay a visit to nearby Paultons Park, family-owned since 1983. Located on the grounds of the former Paultons Estate, it has beautiful landscaping and gardens—and the adorable Peppa Pig World for fans of the cheeky cartoon.

ABOVE: A lavender plant and the grassy lawn outside THE PIG on the beach, located on Dorset's sandy coastline

OPPOSITE: THE PIG at Bridge Place serves a plate of homegrown cured meats, sourdough, olives, and chutney.

THE PIG at Combe, Devon: Located in the East Devon Area of Outstanding Natural Beauty, this hotel puts you within 20 minutes of Exeter and its famous cathedral.

THE PIG at Bridge Place, Kent: Stay here for day trips exploring the small towns and wineries of Kent and Canterbury, just a few miles away. The stained glass windows at Canterbury Cathedral are a draw, as is the history enshrined in Chaucer's *Canterbury Tales*.

THE PIG at Harlyn Bay, Cornwall: To experience a more exclusive part of Cornwall—there is no direct train from London—come here. Plus, the surrounding area has a great restaurant scene.

THE PIG in the South Downs, West Sussex: This 18th-century Georgian house turned polished rural escape is an ideal base for long walks in the rolling hills of South Downs National Park.

BRAEMAR, SCOTLAND, U.K.

THE FIFE ARMS

At this immersive hotel, find a unique blend of Scottish heritage and world-renowned artistry.

YEAR ESTABLISHED: **1856; reopened in 2018** NUMBER OF ROOMS: **46**
FAMOUS FEATURE: **Robust art collection** WHEN TO GO: **May–September**

The vibe at the Fife Arms is Scottish Highlands—defiant and invincible, vast and breathtaking—mixed with high-end artistic vision, plus a few oddities here and there. This is one of the most visually stimulating interiors in the United Kingdom. It's worth booking a dinner reservation here, even if you don't plan to spend the night.

In 1852, Queen Victoria purchased Balmoral Castle, nine miles (14.5 km) from here, pioneering tourism to the town of Braemar, where the Fife Arms first opened in 1856. After a few decades, the Fife Arms became a drab stopover for passers-through. That is until the splashy 2018 reopening by the globally renowned duo behind Swiss art gallery Hauser & Wirth. Among the more than 14,000 pieces of priceless art found at the hotel are works by Pablo Picasso, Lucian Freud, and Louise Bourgeois. The art is deeply thought through and sometimes offbeat. In the Drawing Room, this manifests in classic tartan green walls paired with Zhang Enli's swirly, colorful "Ancient Quartz" on the ceiling, inspired by Scottish agates. And don't miss the Steinway piano turned showstopper art piece.

But art isn't the only thing on the menu. Locals consider the Flying Stag their local pub, where residents and guests are served leveled-up pub favorites like fish-and-chips, beef and ale pie, and sticky toffee pudding. Bertie's Bar, featuring hundreds of bottles of whisky on its shelves, is one of Scotland's top destinations for the drink, and guests can imbibe in tastings in a softly lit space. And perhaps the only place in the Scottish Highlands where heels wouldn't look out of place is Elsa's, a bar at the Fife Arms. This spot for glam

OPPOSITE: The Drawing Room features quintessential Scottish art and antiques, such as the special Fife Arms tartan.

PAGES 68–69: Bagpipers play in front of the Fife Arms during an evening celebration in the village of Braemar.

was inspired by fashion designer Elsa Schiaparelli and her love of pink.

Rooms and suites are divided into categories, starting with the most ornate on the top floor, aptly called the Royal Suites. Nature & Poetry rooms include one inspired by Robert Louis Stevenson, who wrote the first few chapters of *Treasure Island* in Braemar. Scottish Culture rooms pay homage to passions such as astronomy, travel literature, and philosophy. The cozy one-off Artist's Studio with paintbrushes and knickknacks offers the perfect hideaway for writers or artists needing a retreat and inspiration. Those staying in this room may want to book the hotel's three-hour creative writing workshop with a local professional writer and poet. A travel adviser is especially helpful to sort through options here. (You may not want a stag head in your room, for instance.)

The entire stay is immersive, fascinating, and hard to leave, but it's also the perfect launch point for adventure in the Highlands, which can include wild swimming, hikes, fishing, foraging, horseback riding, castle tours, and much more.

But the ultimate souvenir from a Fife Arms stay just might be your own family tartan, designed with a local textile designer.

TIME YOUR TRIP

Queen Elizabeth II loved Braemar because of its proximity to Balmoral, the royal family's estate. She often attended the Braemar Gathering, part of the Highland Games. The games are held the first Saturday of September every year.

EDINBURGH, SCOTLAND, U.K.

THE BALMORAL

All aboard for a stay at this majestic testament to the railroad era.

YEAR ESTABLISHED: **1902** NUMBER OF ROOMS: **167** FAMOUS FEATURE: **The clock tower**
WHEN TO GO: **June–August**

The Balmoral's iconic clock tower, located atop its Victorian facade, has helped people catch their trains for more than a century, always running three minutes ahead of the actual time.

Every year on Hogmanay—aka New Year's Eve—the clock keepers correct the time to ring in the New Year precisely on time. The only exception was in 2020, when they rang in 2021 three minutes early to end the pandemic year faster. After New Year's, the clock is set three minutes ahead to keep locals on time.

Built in 1902 as the railway revolution was under way, The Balmoral was originally known as the North British Railway Station Hotel and sat conveniently next to the main station. In 1991, it reopened as The Balmoral (meaning "majestic dwelling" in Gaelic). Seven years later, Sir Rocco Forte bought the property as the first in a now growing portfolio of hotels. Today, with the Forte family's style behind it—Sir Rocco's sister, Olga Polizzi, is director of design—the hotel feels fresh and inviting, while protecting its history.

Entering the hotel's peaceful environs feels instantly tranquil after a slightly chaotic train station arrival. The best rooms overlook Edinburgh Castle, and it's perfectly situated to visit both New Town and Old Town on foot.

Everything you want from a grand city hotel is here: Michelin-starred dining alongside a casual bar for club sandwich cravings; an indoor pool; and a well-equipped gym. But the soaring Palm Court, with its Venetian chandeliers, is the heart of the hotel. A live harpist provides the soundtrack to an elegant afternoon tea worth booking.

OPPOSITE: Dusk falls over The Balmoral and the statue of Arthur Wellesley, the first duke of Wellington, in Edinburgh.

SUNNMØRE REGION, NORWAY

62° NORD COLLECTION

From hotel to hotel, explore this picturesque part of Norway in luxury and style.

YEAR ESTABLISHED: **1891** NUMBER OF ROOMS: **Varies by property** FAMOUS FEATURE: **Experiential itinerary**
WHEN TO GO: **April–June**

Founded by Knut Flakk and his wife, Line, 62° Nord is an experiential travel company and collection of hotels that personalizes itineraries to fit this cinematic region. The producers of *Frozen* visited the area, which is said to have inspired the look of the Kingdom of Arendelle, and so did production teams for HBO's *Succession* and the 2021 James Bond film *No Time to Die*. Depending on guests' interests, an itinerary might include road or e-bikes, skiing, hiking, cruises, wild swimming, saunas, and more. And the fjord-to-lobby style of travel makes these itineraries unique.

The jumping-off point for all itineraries is Ålesund (a short flight from Oslo, Copenhagen, or Amsterdam), perhaps the prettiest village in Norway. Ålesund faces the open sea, with access to puffin and seal colonies and the fjords beyond. After a fire destroyed 90 percent of the town in 1904, it was rebuilt with more than 50 Norwegian architects contributing creative design. Their work was inspired by the art nouveau style popular in Germany at the time and partly financed by Kaiser Wilhelm II, who loved the area.

Many guests begin at **Hotel Brosundet,** a former fishing warehouse turned small-town retreat with a soaring fireplace and excellent breakfast buffet. The best rooms have views of Aksla Mountain—it's worth the 418-step climb to its peak for a sweeping view of Ålesund. One of the most photographed landmarks in town is the small, red Molja Lighthouse, which doubles as Room 47

AFTER CHECK-IN

In the 1980s, Knut Flakk's father bought Devold of Norway, a wool and knitwear company with roots dating to 1853. His daughter Maria Lilly Flakk started a new luxury line, O.A.D., using all-natural fibers like Norwegian wool, mohair, and silk in more contemporary styles.

OPPOSITE: A chef picks fresh greens from the garden for a meal at Hotel Union Øye.

PAGES 74–75: An aerial view of Hotel Brosundet (yellow and white buildings on water) in the idyllic, snowy town of Ålesund

HOTEL BROSUNDET
T. BERSET

of the hotel (breakfast is delivered in a basket).

Directly from the Brosundet, a boat whisks you to **Hotel Union Øye,** located on the shore of the beautiful Hjørundfjord. The hotel has played a huge role in keeping this small fjord village alive.

The hotel has hosted luminaries like Karen Blixen and Sir Arthur Conan Doyle. Check in here and the reception desk and fireplace will make you feel like you've stepped back in time to the building's opening year of 1891. Union Øye's gardens were designed by a top Norwegian landscaper, and its restaurant tasting menus are sourced from local produce. You'll find yourself craving the slow pace of life as soon as you leave one of the world's great belle epoque hospitality treasures.

The next stop is **Storfjord Hotel.** If you have a car during your stay here, a stunning drive reaches the famous (and heavily trafficked) UNESCO-listed Geirangerfjord, a perfectly carved fjord and a must-see. At 62° Nord, guests are directed on less trampled paths: Drive to Hellesylt and take a one-hour car ferry to Geiranger.

ALTERNATE STAY

Spend at least two nights in Oslo on either end of your trip. The city feels like a futuristic, ever evolving Scandi capital. Stay at Sommerro House or Amerikalinjen. Don't miss the extraordinary murals inside Oslo City Hall (Rådhus), where the Nobel Peace Prize is awarded every December 10 and locals often get married. Walk the buzzy neighborhood of Grünerløkka for locally owned cafés and shops.

ABOVE: **Storfjord Hotel closely partners with local farms and beverage producers to serve the freshest, finest meals to its guests.**

OPPOSITE: **After fishing in Ålesund, let the chefs at Apotekergata No. 5 prepare your catch of the day.**

Storfjord, built in 2006, is a dreamy, slow-paced showcase of Norwegian tradition with one of the best hotel views in the world overlooking the fjord. Its location also makes it a prime kayaking and hiking spot. Rooms and public spaces are divided among log cabin–style buildings, which also feature a wooden sauna and hot tubs. Relaxation is forefront here, with candlestick lighting and plush seating throughout. Try the local brewery's signature Storfjord Brygg, made for the hotel.

For now, none of the 62° Nord hotels have gyms, but that's okay. Follow the Norwegian way: Nature makes for the best workout. Keep in mind, the weather can be variable, and spring is your best shot at sunny days.

It's just 30 minutes from Storfjord back to Ålesund and its small but excellent airport.

STOCKHOLM, SWEDEN

ETT HEM

This trio of town houses makes for a cozy, homelike stay in a bustling yet charming city center.

YEAR ESTABLISHED: 2012 **NUMBER OF ROOMS:** 22 **FAMOUS FEATURE:** Home-away-from-home spaces
WHEN TO GO: March–June

If you ask hotel lovers around the world about their favorite properties, one hotel seems to inspire the most adulation: Ett Hem in Stockholm. Its name means "a home," and while many hotels claim to "feel like home," this one actually delivers.

The first Ett Hem town house was built in 1910 as a private residence in Stockholm's Östermalm; it opened as a hotel with just 12 rooms in 2012. In 2022, 10 new rooms were added in two adjacent townhomes—all in collaboration with star designer Ilse Crawford.

"I live in a similar house that I bought years ago and the idea started then, though I didn't take it seriously," says owner Jeanette Mix. Eventually, that thought became Ett Hem, a dream realized. "We have kept the heart of these former homes—it truly is like you are in someone's house."

Sitting in the hotel's public spaces, you want to get to know Mix. The town houses are an extension of her stylish eye, inspired by her own travels and interest in food, fashion, design, art, and culture. Extraordinary furniture in a mix of patterns and colors somehow comes together to feel supremely comfortable—not quite perfect, but perfectly top-quality.

"I am not trying to trick or fool my guests," Mix says. "I don't cheat anywhere on quality, from the handmade ceramics to the quality of the paneling and the shampoo in the rooms. I genuinely want the guests to experience the best, for all the daily rituals of a hotel stay."

Nearly 20 chefs create the food at Ett Hem, where every single dish is locally

OPPOSITE: Step inside the oasis of Ett Hem's courtyard garden to relax or chat with a travel companion.

PAGES 80–81: The beautiful hotel rooms at Ett Hem feature both modern and classic design elements.

sourced or handmade, including the jams, granola, and bread. Freshly baked cakes and coffee await for afternoon *fika* (the local coffee break).

Each corner of the hotel brings delightful discoveries. Guests roam and settle as they wish into cozy seats by a fireplace or a table in the greenhouse with open doors that lead out to the beautiful gardens (unusual in Stockholm's city center). The library's books are personally curated, and the residents' lounge has a grand piano. The kitchen community table is for coming together with guests of all ages, genders, and social groups in an informal setting.

Though leaving the property might be hard to imagine, from Ett Hem, the city's core is wonderfully walkable and is a bastion of Scandinavian ideal living. Stockholm is made up of 14 islands connected by bridges with a mix of historic buildings and museums, green parks, and waterways.

AFTER CHECK-IN

The afternoon coffee break tradition of *fika* is a national pastime in Sweden and is best accompanied by a Swedish bun. The classics are cardamom and cinnamon, sprinkled with pearl sugar; in November, you'll see saffron buns pop up on menus. Try local favorite bakeries like Lillebrors Bageri, Stora Bageriet, and Socker Sucker.

COPENHAGEN, DENMARK

HOTEL D'ANGLETERRE

This iconic Denmark hotel is as much a part of the country's history as fairy tales and Legos.

YEAR ESTABLISHED: **1755** NUMBER OF ROOMS: **92** FAMOUS FEATURE: **Danish elegance**
WHEN TO GO: **April–May or September**

For many visitors, Copenhagen inspires visions of an alternate reality: It is a fairy-tale city, a coffee and bun lover's dream, where you feel totally at ease. Don't be surprised if you find yourself looking up real estate sites to check apartment prices.

Until you can buy real estate, you'll find no better base than the Hotel d'Angleterre, one of Europe's grande dames overlooking Copenhagen's grandest square, also home to the annual Christmas market. The hotel is a five-minute walk from Nyhavn, with the postcard lineup of colorful houses Copenhagen is known for. One of the city's most famous residents, Hans Christian Andersen, author of "The Little Mermaid" and other beloved fairy tales, stayed and wrote at the Hotel d'Angleterre.

The original hotel first opened in 1755, but was destroyed by a massive fire. The hotel was rebuilt in 1795 and has become part of Danish history. When you walk into reception, you see an Andy Warhol painting of Queen Margrethe II and an incredible Lego model of the hotel. Many more Danish artists feature throughout the property, where the public spaces are comfortable and chic. A glittering champagne bar is a local gathering spot.

Rent one of the hotel's bikes to experience Copenhagen—one of the best biking cities in the world. Use two wheels to hunt for some of the city's amazing buns (Juno Bakery and Hart Bageri are two favorites).

ALTERNATE STAY

The Nimb Hotel overlooks Tivoli Gardens, Copenhagen's historic, magical, and twinkly-lit amusement park. As a guest of the hotel, you have access to Tivoli before it opens. Take advantage because there is nowhere like it in the world: The rides are secondary to the lush gardens and dozens of restaurants. The hotel is as whimsical as the park and features one of the best watering holes in the city, Nimb Bar.

OPPOSITE: A family enjoys breakfast at the Hotel d'Angleterre.

LUCERNE, SWITZERLAND

HOTEL SCHWEIZERHOF

Having stood the test of time, this fifth-generation hotel embraces its yesteryear vibe and scenic setting.

YEAR ESTABLISHED: **1845** NUMBER OF ROOMS: **101** FAMOUS FEATURE: **Lake views** WHEN TO GO: **Year-round**

Lucerne, Switzerland, is one of the most romantic cities in the world, and the Hotel Schweizerhof, now owned by the fifth generation of the charming Hauser family, is the grande dame.

Schweizerhof is an icon that hasn't been taken over by technology. With so many hotels succumbing to the latest tech, it's endearing that here the light switches turn on and off without using a tablet; the elevator is a time warp with velvet seats and wood panels; and the wood floors still creak a bit. The breakfast buffet is served in a historic ballroom with chandeliers. The lobby, which features original tiles and columns, and the sunny terrace (the place to be in the summer) remain reassuringly the same year after year—as do many of the staff, who exemplify Swiss warmth and swift hospitality.

From the hotel, guests can take in all of Switzerland's natural beauty in one view: snow-covered mountains, the well-preserved Old Town with colorful buildings and cobblestoned squares, and a sparkling lake where swans glide over translucent water. Lake-facing rooms include panoramas of Mount Pilatus (one of the region's most popular day trips), Bürgenstock mountain, and historic paddle steamboats from the early 1900s chugging their way into port. Don't miss Tuesday and Saturday mornings by Chapel Bridge, a symbol of the city, for the Lucerne farmers market. It becomes the central meeting point for locals in town.

OPPOSITE: The glowing exterior of the Hotel Schweizerhof, one of the finest five-star stays in the city of Lucerne

SCHWEIZERHOF
SCHWEIZERHOF

ASCONA, SWITZERLAND

HOTEL EDEN ROC ASCONA

Food and well-being are highlights of this Italian-Swiss hybrid on Lake Maggiore.

YEAR ESTABLISHED: **1971** NUMBER OF ROOMS: **95** FAMOUS FEATURE: **Good-for-you cuisine** WHEN TO GO: **April–October**

Ascona still feels like a bit of a secret. In this small town on Lake Maggiore in Ticino, the Italian-speaking region of Switzerland, Swiss efficiency meets Italian passion. And the most glamorous place to stay here is the Hotel Eden Roc, designed by Carlo Rampazzi, who was actually born in Ascona, where his brother was the mayor for many years. Hotel Eden Roc feels like a direct extension of Rampazzi's personality—nothing is subtle about the design choices; it is unequivocally fun and charismatic.

Upon arrival, start with an alfresco lunch at Marina for a great view of the lake. Hotel Eden Roc Ascona is owned by a Swiss hotel group, the Tschuggen Collection, which is known for its "Moving Mountains" guest experience programs. Look for the program's "Nourish" symbol on menus; it means a dish is locally sourced, plant-based, and nutrient-rich. For instance, start the day with buckwheat waffles with pine nuts and spinach, which is just as delicious as it is good for you. Of course, there is always a cake available by the slice and local cheese from Ticino.

On the cocktail menu, try the Operation Sunrise. From the bar, look out to the *casetta* (little house). As the menu states: "On March 19, 1945, during the bank holiday San Giuseppe, the Operation Sunrise took place in Ascona and precisely in our casetta which put an end to the hostilities of World War II."

Sounds like there is a movie ready to be made at the Eden Roc—but let's still try to keep Ascona our little secret while we can.

AFTER CHECK-IN

From the hotel, the main lakeside promenade is just a three-minute walk away. Walk all the way down to find the red "Grand Tour of Switzerland" sign for the best photo op. Beloved local favorite Osteria Nostrana occupies three buildings with lots of outdoor seating from which you can enjoy lake views. Walk up Via Borgo, a main shopping street.

OPPOSITE: Take in majestic views of Lake Maggiore from Eden Bar's terrace.

ZERMATT, SWITZERLAND

MONT CERVIN PALACE

Matterhorn views are just part of the draw to this Alpine retreat.

YEAR ESTABLISHED: **1852** NUMBER OF ROOMS: **150** FAMOUS FEATURE: **Terrace views of Matterhorn**
WHEN TO GO: **July–September**

Of all the Alpine villages, Zermatt—and its mighty Matterhorn (emblematic of Switzerland itself)—is perhaps the most iconic. The village is famed for mountaineering, hiking, skiing, nightlife, and great restaurants. Part of its magic is in the arrival: The train ride from Visp to Zermatt is just over an hour with mountain paradise views at every curve on the upward tracks.

The sharp-peaked Matterhorn, which rises 14,692 feet (4,478 m) above sea level, can be temperamental, hiding behind ever changing light patterns and clouds that refuse to lift. But when the clouds do part and reveal the peak, Matterhorn asserts a magnetic pull, making it hard to look away.

At Mont Cervin Palace, Zermatt's cozy and traditional icon, you can settle in for a long haul of peak-gazing from your room's geranium-lined terrace. Out of 150 rooms, 61 boast Matterhorn views. In the early morning hours, you can see the faraway headlights of early risers attempting to scale the summit.

The Seiler brothers first leased Mont Cervin Palace in 1857 and officially bought it in 1867, two years after the first ascent of the Matterhorn by Brit Edward Whymper and his team. Though the descent was tragic (four people died), the little village shot to great fame after the expedition, and Mont Cervin found a rapt and steady flow of travelers. Today, the hotel is part of

AFTER CHECK-IN

Chez Vrony remains the ultimate Alpine lunch spot with a Matterhorn view, accessible by foot from Sunnegga in the summer or by skiing in the winter.

OPPOSITE: Stay at Mont Cervin Palace for easy access to the ample ski slopes near the mighty Matterhorn.

PAGES 90–91: Set in a valley beneath the Swiss Alps, Mont Cervin Palace is close to the old village center and the great outdoors.

MONT
CERVIN

Michel Reybier Hospitality, which also owns the historic Monte Rosa (Whymper's base before his ascent) and the Schweizerhof, a cozy four-star option with a fondue restaurant on the main street.

Despite its age and rich history, at Mont Cervin, nothing is ostentatious. The vibe throughout is warm and inviting mountain luxury. Rooms are chalet style, with dark woods and soft blankets. The spa has a large indoor/outdoor pool, plus a shallow children's paddling pool (and a lovely playroom for kids, too). And there are welcoming restaurants and bars throughout. (The hotel's sushi place across the street is a welcome change from classic Alpine fare.)

Zermatt is technically car free, but don't be fooled—small electric vehicles zealously zoom around town. Historic horse-drawn red carriages pick up Mont Cervin guests at the train station, even though it's a five-minute walk to the lobby.

If your goal while visiting is to experience Matterhorn for yourself, three lift stations and cable cars allow you to access different parts of the mountain: Sunnegga; Furi up to Glacier Paradise; and the historic Gornergrat Bahn, the first electric cogwheel railway in Europe and a must for most visitors, especially train buffs. Have a slice of apple strudel at the Gornergrat's café. Other top sights include the Gorner Gorge and the Five Lakes loop walk.

Take note: The hotel is typically closed from mid-April through mid-June and again from mid-October through mid-December.

ZURICH, SWITZERLAND

THE WIDDER

Old meets new at this boutique hotel known for its finery and food.

YEAR ESTABLISHED: **1995** NUMBER OF ROOMS: **49** FAMOUS FEATURE: **Michelin-starred restaurant**
WHEN TO GO: **Year-round**

Just off Bahnhofstrasse, Zurich's main shopping street, is a cobblestoned slope to the Widder, a collection of nine 15th-century town houses turned into a very special boutique hotel.

It took a decade and a team of 1,000 conservationists and designers to meld past and present in what is now the Widder. Historic elements such as stone walls and wooden beams blend seamlessly with the glass-and-steel elevators and passageways that connect the townhomes. Each room is unique but includes some design signatures, like black-and-white-striped chairs, geometric carpets, and patterned wooden floors and desks. A small lobby leads out to the popular Widder Garden, which is open from April until around October, when the weather begins to change.

The hotel also features some of the city's best dining options, open to anyone, guest or not. Find a Michelin-starred fine dining option as well as a casual burger joint and an award-winning bar. The Widder is part of the small Living Circle hotel group, which prioritizes local farms and sourcing from nature; everything is top-quality. Try the Swiss Bircher muesli (named after Swiss physician Maximilian Bircher-Benner) for breakfast. (Tip: Book a table at nearby sister hotel Storchen's Terrace La Rôtisserie for beautiful riverside terrace views. The terrace stays open from April to October, weather permitting.)

Zurich is walkable and compact, and it's all just outside the hotel's doors, starting with Lindenhof Hill for the best view of Old Town and Grossmünster church. Everywhere you look, the distinct Swiss flag—red with a white cross—is flying.

ALTERNATE STAY

Switzerland's long tradition of hospitality means you'll find a number of top hotels in Zurich, including the seventh-generation-owned Baur au Lac and maritime-inspired La Réserve Eden au Lac. The spectacular Dolder Grand (see page 155), an urban retreat overlooking the city, was built in 1899. For less expensive options in Old Town, look at the Marktgasse Hotel and the Hotel Adler (though you might smell fondue in the rooms). The hip 25Hours Hotel on Langstrasse is set in the buzzy Europaallee neighborhood.

OPPOSITE: **After a day exploring Zurich, enjoy a cocktail at the Widder Bar.**

PARIS, FRANCE

RELAIS CHRISTINE

Its cozy charm in the City of Light makes this getaway a must for Paris regulars.

YEAR ESTABLISHED: **1979** NUMBER OF ROOMS: **48** FAMOUS FEATURE: **Private garden** WHEN TO GO: **Year-round**

Distinctly Parisian, the charming and beloved Relais Christine hotel is tucked away on a quiet street, between Saint-Germain-des-Prés and the Latin Quarter, two neighborhoods that have long attracted writers and artists. With just two restaurants and a sweet little cinema on the street, the location could not be better for escaping the crowds while within walking distance of every major Parisian attraction (including Notre-Dame Cathedral, the Louvre, the Jardin du Luxembourg, and the Marais).

Built on the remains of a 13th-century abbey in 1898 to reflect 17th- and 18th-century Parisian architecture, the hotel preserves many historical details of the Left Bank town house turned hotel. For instance, the Guerlain Spa is built within the abbey's old vaults.

You enter Relais Christine—owned by the same French family since 1979—from a private courtyard where the sound of birds evokes the French countryside. The top Garden Suites open up to a private garden in the back of the property, where the team harvests honey from hidden beehives. Like a family home, the lounge—adorned in deep blue tones, bookshelves, soft seating, and a fireplace—invites you to stay a while (the honor bar doesn't hurt, either).

Not one of the hotel's 48 rooms and suites is the same, but each boasts a mix of French antiques, cozy fabrics, and marble bathrooms (with Diptyque amenities) and a range of color palettes, from neutrals to vibrant hues and floral prints. The same designer worked on both Relais Christine and its sister

ALTERNATE STAY

Hotel du Danube in Paris is a wonderful three-star option a stone's throw from famous cafés Les Deux Magots and Café de Flore in the 6th arrondissement. Family-owned since 1962, the hotel is a find discreetly shared with friends for its charm and value.

OPPOSITE: Tucked away in Paris's 16th arrondissement, find the breathtaking facade of Saint James.

PAGES 96–97: A Deluxe Junior Suite at the Relais Christine is a lavish retreat fit for two or three people.

property, Saint James Paris, which make for an ideal combination for two stays in Paris.

Located in the residential 16th arrondissement, a 15-minute walk from the Eiffel Tower, Saint James Paris is a great choice for visitors seeking a quiet but grand retreat. It's the only château hotel in Paris that transports you to the countryside, with whimsical, bold interiors.

For families with young kids, the pool in the Guerlain Spa adds major bonus points, while the wood-paneled bar is the perfect grown-up spot for drinks before dinner or for working during the day. The bar is also open to the public after 7 p.m. and is a wonderful way to get a glimpse of the decor.

Back at the Relais Christine, there is no main on-site restaurant, encouraging you to explore the culinary abundance that is Paris. But a generous breakfast buffet focuses on French products. "It's important for our guests to discover French cheeses," one staffer says. The hotel offers room service with the classics (club sandwiches, omelets), but it also works with two neighborhood restaurants—the refined Le Christine and Chez Fernand—to offer bistro icons like beef bourguignon.

DRINK IT UP

Paris has some of the most beautiful palace hotels in the world, among them Le Bristol, La Réserve, Four Seasons Hotel George V, and Le Meurice—all worth visiting for a drink or dining, even if you're not staying the night.

CÔTE D'AZUR, FRANCE

GRAND-HÔTEL DU CAP-FERRAT

From pool parties to grand views, this escape on the edge of the sea offers the gold standard of luxury.

YEAR ESTABLISHED: 1908 **NUMBER OF ROOMS: 74** **FAMOUS FEATURE: Olympic-size pool**
WHEN TO GO: May–July

It has been a concerted effort to not overuse the word "heaven" in this book. Many hotels could qualify as a literal place of complete bliss, delight, and peace. But the descriptor is apt in the blissful Côte d'Azur in the South of France, where sun-dappled light seems to act like a filter, perfecting every view. That same light has inspired legions of artists like Matisse, Picasso, Renoir, and Chagall, who all visited the region.

Cap Ferrat, one of the most expensive enclaves in the world, is a peninsula of hills and cliffs jutting out into the Mediterranean. Set within the backdrop of one of Cap Ferrat's most magnificent views is the Grand-Hôtel du Cap-Ferrat, now managed by Four Seasons. And though the hotel offers the ultimate in luxury, the service is warm and never snobby. One guest raved about it as the "gold standard" of French Riviera hotels.

Built in 1909, the light-filled rotunda—just beyond the reception desk—was designed by Gustave Eiffel, who completed the Eiffel Tower in the 1880s. Panoramic views are found throughout the hotel. A grand staircase leads out from the rotunda and down to a path cutting through 17 acres (7 ha) of gardens that scent the air like perfume. The French flag waves above the iconic typeface carved across the top of the hotel's white exterior.

Its crowning design achievement, however, is one of the most incredible

OPPOSITE: Book a private dinner in the gorgeous garden at Grand-Hôtel du Cap-Ferrat.

PAGES 100–101: The enchanting pool and grounds of Villa Beauchamp, a five-bedroom villa that is part of the hotel

hotel pools in the world. Meander down to the pool from shaded paths or take the funicular to the Olympic-size beauty overlooking the water. Like any great hotel, characters are woven into its story, like famous swim instructor Pierre Gruneberg, who first spotted the property while hiking at age 18 and went on to teach swim classes here for more than 70 years. The torch has been passed to a new fitness coach and swim instructor, who encourage guests to be active while on holiday.

Though the property has attracted the glitterati since it opened, it has other historic stories to tell, too. In 1914, it doubled as a WWI hospital, and during WWII, it closed for six years.

Rooms are oversize, and a sea view is worth splurging for, if possible, though you're never far from a view. Pool suites are more contemporary in style, with indoor/outdoor living. Families needing space often book one of the three villa options. You can debate its merits, but Netflix's *Emily in Paris* filmed a showstopper scene in one of the hotel's top sea-view suites.

CLOSE BY

Most visitors fly into Nice Côte d'Azur Airport, about 45 minutes from Cap Ferrat. Spend a night or two in Nice at Hotel Negresco, the grande dame since 1913 with colorful art and furnishings and a stunning chandelier in the historic Royal Reception rotunda. Hôtel La Pérouse is a quirky and charming boutique option within walking distance of the Old Town.

PARIS, FRANCE

J.K. PLACE, PARIS

This beloved boutique hotel with an Italian soul makes its global mark in the City of Light.

YEAR ESTABLISHED: **2020** NUMBER OF ROOMS: **29** FAMOUS FEATURE: **Italian vibes in Paris**
WHEN TO VISIT: **Year-round**

A five-minute walk from the Musée d'Orsay, J.K. Place, Paris sets you up to become a Parisian flaneur and return to what feels like your very own pied-à-terre.

The small collection of J.K. hotels—named for Jonathan Kafri, father of Ori Kafri, CEO and co-founder—is built on a very specific philosophy, one that mimics a tailor crafting made-to-measure clothing: "To go to a tailor, spend time, look at the fabric, try it on, you create a connection that you cannot copy and paste," Kafri says. "We try to emphasize the human aspect of it. We are looking after you. You need a little bit of romance, a little bit of love to be in this industry."

Occupying the former Norwegian Embassy, J.K. Place has turned the building into a plush hideaway. Designer Michele Bönan sourced one-of-a-kind pieces from Parisian markets; everything here is refined and cozy with soft lighting and lush furnishings (settle in for an espresso); coffee-table books are stacked everywhere.

You'll find everything you need on the property: a subterranean spa and small pool; a bar to order signature spritzes; and a delicious Italian restaurant built in a light-filled space that offers a welcome contrast to Parisian indulgence with green juices and egg-white omelets. And feel free to open the minibar—it's all included in the rate.

This is J.K.'s first venture outside of Italy, and it quickly has become a Parisian icon. Guests are thankful—they want something like J.K. wherever they go, tailored to them.

AFTER CHECK-IN

Like a choose-your-own-adventure book, the streets of Paris await your arrival. Saint-Germain's café culture is to the left of the hotel on your way out; Le Bon Marché and the Eiffel Tower to the right. On Sunday mornings, don't miss the organic market, Marché Raspail, which offers the best produce imaginable, plus French cheeses, olives, baguettes, eggs, and yogurt—the scent of rotisserie chickens turning, flavoring the potatoes below, is in the air.

OPPOSITE: The living room at J.K. Place melds Italian flair with Parisian elegance.

CHANEL
FRENCH STYLE

ROQUEBRUNE-CAP-MARTIN, FRANCE

THE MAYBOURNE RIVIERA

In a region of glitz and glam, this sleek hotel spares no expense.

YEAR ESTABLISHED: **2021** NUMBER OF ROOMS: **69** FAMOUS FEATURE: **Sea views** WHEN TO GO: **April–September**

When it opened in 2021, the Maybourne Riviera instantly became a new legend on a legendary coast. Born from a hotel group that owns some of the world's most iconic properties—Claridge's, the Connaught, and the Berkeley in London—the Maybourne Riviera trades afternoon tea for afternoon rosé by the infinity pool on bright orange sun loungers.

Located 15 minutes from the center of Monte Carlo, the Maybourne Riviera has endless views of sky and sea—and of tiny, built-up, yacht-filled Monaco. Being famously moneyed—with many residents into the billions—no expense has been spared at this hotel. The exterior is gloriously modernist with windows and sharp lines, reigning over—and literally in—the rocky cliffs of Roquebrune-Cap-Martin, a peninsula where creatives in art and food have long found inspiration.

The hotel itself is filled with extraordinary pieces of art. The lobby ceiling, for instance, is dominated by the embracing figures of Louise Bourgeois's aluminum sculpture "The Couple." All of the oversize rooms have terraces and extraordinary sea views; there is also a sleek spa.

Michelin-starred chef Mauro Colagreco runs two restaurants here: Ceto, which focuses on seasonality and sustainability, and the Riviera Restaurant, which explores the unique terroir of the Riviera. This is the hotel that cemented the Maybourne Hotel Group as a global power player beyond the U.K.—just watch for what's to come.

ALTERNATE STAYS

In the center of Monte Carlo, visit the Hôtel de Paris, open since 1864 and loved by Coco Chanel. The glittering two-floor Princess Grace Suite pays homage to Grace Kelly, who left Hollywood to marry Prince Rainier and is forever intertwined with Monaco's history.

OPPOSITE: **At first glance, it appears the Maybourne Riviera's infinity pool spills into the Mediterranean Sea.**

CANNES, FRANCE

CARLTON CANNES

Movie and celebrity history was made at this classic hotel in a city that knows how to celebrate film.

YEAR ESTABLISHED: 1913 **NUMBER OF ROOMS:** 332 **FAMOUS FEATURE:** Location on La Croisette
WHEN TO GO: March–May

The Carlton Cannes stands in the center of La Croisette, one of the best promenades in the world curving along the Mediterranean Sea. With its famed two-domed, cream-colored exterior, framed by palm trees and (usually) a bright blue Riviera sky, the hotel was classified as a historical monument in 1989. Thank goodness the oft photographed exterior did not change during a 2022 transformation by Regent Hotels, but the interior has been reimagined, its history preserved with a bright and airy modern edge. During the remodeling, a parking lot became a swimming pool and garden; layers of paint were stripped away to reveal original marble; and new glass chandeliers were hung in public spaces.

Alfred Hitchcock chose the Carlton as the setting for his classic 1955 *To Catch a Thief,* the ultimate travelogue for the French Riviera. During filming, Grace Kelly met her future husband, Prince Rainier of Monaco, and the course of her life changed dramatically. Today, you can stay in the Alfred Hitchcock Suite where they filmed the movie's kiss scene. The suite is also famous for its panoramic views of the bay of Cannes and the Estérel.

The Carlton Beach Club is a perennial hot spot, and nothing beats a Nicoise salad with a cold glass of rosé, craning your neck to see who has just arrived.

ALTERNATE STAY

Two other historic hotels line La Croisette: the glamorous Hotel Barrière Le Majestic Cannes, right across from the Palais des Festivals, where Cannes Film Festival attendees preview new films every May, and the Hôtel Martinez, an art deco masterpiece.

OPPOSITE: Olivier Revel, the proud chief doorman, poses in front of the Carlton Cannes.

CARLTON
ROLEX

PROVENCE, FRANCE

VILLA LA COSTE

Artwork peppers the grounds of this villa-style hotel, which stands out from the quaint Provençal digs of the area.

YEAR ESTABLISHED: **2016** NUMBER OF ROOMS: **28** FAMOUS FEATURE: **Artwork**
WHEN TO GO: **March–October**

Villa La Coste is extraordinary, set within the 600-acre (243 ha) rolling hills of Château La Coste, dotted with tall cypress trees, olive trees, and vineyards. Even so, the hotel is second to the immersive, art-filled grounds.

"I consider this to be one of the most incredible contemporary art experiences that exists in the world today," says Melissa Biggs Bradley, founder of boutique travel company Indagare.

If you're seeking classic Provençal-style farmhouse chic with antiques and exposed timber and a palette of florals and lavender inspired by the fields, this isn't it. But the hotel provides one of the most unique hospitality experiences in Europe and was started as a passion project by longtime hotelier Paddy McKillen, who bought it shortly after seeing it. "The day I came to Château La Coste for the first time, I was overwhelmed," he says. "I was moved by the beauty."

What makes this hotel unique is its art collection. Throughout the hotel are more than 30 major artworks as well as architectural pavilions by the likes of Tadao Ando, Jean Nouvel, and Frank Gehry. There are also sculptures by Alexander Calder and Louise Bourgeois (one signature spider sculpture, hovering over a pond, is particularly striking).

"The Oscar Niemeyer Pavilion absolutely blows me away," says Bradley. "It was the famous architect's last big project before he died at age 104."

The grounds are open for outside guests to explore in several ways, from

OPPOSITE: A Michelin-starred chef curates fine appetizers, entrées, and desserts for guests at Villa La Coste.

PAGES 110–111: Guests find relaxation and peace during their stay at Villa La Coste, a boutique retreat nestled in the heart of Provence.

wine tastings in the chateau's cave to two-hour guided tours of the sculptures for less than 30 euros a person. Dining options are housed in museum-quality buildings, most impressively the glass-and-concrete café by Tadao Ando. The only European outpost of Argentine chef Francis Mallmann is here, as is fine dining by three-Michelin-starred chef Hélène Darroze.

If you stay overnight, all the villa suites feel oversize, with entry-level rooms that start out at around 1,000 square feet (93 m^2). The two-bedroom villas feature private pools. Both options have floor-to-ceiling sliding glass doors that allow for indoor/outdoor living and views to the Luberon Valley.

Of course, Provence—though known for pastoral delights—also offers some of the best small urban cultural experiences in the world. Thirty minutes from the hotel is Aix-en-Provence, where Cézanne was born and died. In Arles, you can walk in the footsteps of Van Gogh, who spent more than two years in Provence, and see where he painted some of his most famous works, including "Starry Night Over the Rhône" and "The Yellow House," depicting where he lived.

AFTER CHECK-IN

Arles boasts an impressive number of Roman ruins, and because cars are banned in town, walking around is a joy. Arles is also an arts and culture hub based on its connection to Van Gogh. Some of Melissa Biggs Bradley's favorites include the Parc des Ateliers, the Musée Réattu, Fondation Vincent van Gogh Arles, and Lee Ufan Arles.

HAMBURG, GERMANY

THE FONTENAY

Within walking distance of Hamburg's top attraction, this Zen-inspired hotel offers an oasis in the city.

YEAR ESTABLISHED: **2018** NUMBER OF ROOMS: **131** FAMOUS FEATURE: **Feng shui design**
WHEN TO GO: **May–September**

Though it is Germany's second largest city and biggest port, Hamburg has traditionally trailed behind creative Berlin and party city Munich in its appeal to travelers. But in 2017, the Elbphilharmonie, a spectacular 2,100-seat concert hall with a reflective glass facade, opened in the city's historic working harbor and immediately attracted a new crowd.

A year later, The Fontenay opened, a perfect complement to the modern Elbphilharmonie on the edge of the Alstersee, a lake in the heart of the city. The hotel is a 10-minute walk to the city center and a 15-minute drive to the Elbphilharmonie.

Architect Jan Störmer created a modern sculptural masterpiece, a design that not only follows the principles of feng shui but also mimics the fluid lines of the lake with circular forms joining together to create public spaces, courtyards, and an 89-foot-high (27 m) glass atrium. The exterior is pure white, with a dirt-resistant enamel coating. At The Fontenay Spa, day visitors and hotel guests enjoy panoramic views from the sauna and indoor/outdoor pool. On the sixth floor, a perennially popular spot for locals, the rooftop bar has the best view of Hamburg and the lake.

While you're here, consider a visit or a stay at the Fairmont Hotel Vier Jahreszeiten, open since 1897. The five-star hotel is the city's grande dame and has a more traditional look and multiple restaurants, including the modern Condi Lounge, a great spot to grab a coffee and praline to enjoy on the adjacent sun terrace.

MORE TO DO

With pristine views and incredible seafood, Sylt, Germany's northernmost island, has been compared to the Hamptons. Within walking distance of the beach and the village of Keitum is superstylish and comfortable Severin's Resort & Spa, built with thatched roofs and an extensive spa.

OPPOSITE: The Atrium Lounge, with its 89-foot-high (27 m) ceilings, is the centerpiece of The Fontenay in Hamburg.

BAVARIA, GERMANY

SCHLOSS ELMAU

A retreat for creatives for more than a century, this wellness escape offers views, spas, and performances.

YEAR ESTABLISHED: 1916 **NUMBER OF ROOMS:** 162 **FAMOUS FEATURE:** Music performances
WHEN TO GO: June–September

Much more than a hotel, Schloss Elmau is a spectacular, soul-stirring cultural retreat on the Austrian-Bavarian border, between Munich and Innsbruck deep in a private valley below the Alps. This is a lesser known European dreamscape. Though it doesn't boast big-ticket names like the Dolomites or Tuscany, the mountain air is soothing, and the scenery is abundant with glacial lakes, rivers, streams, and high peaks.

Run with humor and passion by hotelier and tech entrepreneur Dietmar Mueller-Elmau, the castle was originally opened in 1916 by his grandfather. "He was a very famous writer," Mueller-Elmau says, "and the idea was to create a retreat for his readers to take a vacation from self, free from ideology, and just be with nature." It was an immediate draw. The valley has been a center for music, literature, and art for more than 100 uninterrupted years, even during WWII, when the army confiscated the hotel.

Mueller-Elmau's grandfather also built a beautiful concert hall with some of the best acoustics in the world, bringing hundreds of musicians to the valley. Unfortunately, a 2005 fire destroyed almost everything except for this historic hall, which remains the heart of the resort, hosting some 200 concerts a year.

The extensive cultural calendar tempts almost every guest, though you can also choose to just sit and enjoy the Alpine views. "Our philosophy is freedom of choice, letting everyone do what they want," says Mueller-Elmau. Aside from nightly jazz in the bar and one-off concerts, the slate of music

AFTER CHECK-IN

From June to September, you can enjoy a three-hour hike along the King's Way from the Elmau Valley to visit Schachen House, originally a retreat for King Ludwig II. In the middle of pristine nature, it is an extravagant world of contradiction, where the Far East meets Bavaria in decor.

OPPOSITE: Relax in the luxurious sauna at Shantigiri Adult Spa and admire the striking natural beauty of Bavaria.

PAGES 116–117: The glittering resort of Schloss Elmau is tucked beneath the towering Bavarian Alps.

events includes festivals for classical (in November) and chamber (in January) performances. The magical—and likely largest in the world—hotel bookshop hosts author readings and talks and boasts a large children's section.

There are now two distinct places to stay at Schloss Elmau. After the fire, Mueller-Elmau took over ownership and first opened the Hideaway, a "luxury spa retreat and cultural hideaway" with 115 rooms. The 47-room Retreat opened in 2015 with political summits in mind—it famously hosted the G7 that year and again in 2022. To avoid VIP squabbling, the hotel offers six identical presidential suites, plus a separate "west wing" for the American president. "It seems like you're in the middle of nowhere, and I think this makes it the best place to debate the problems of the world," Mueller-Elmau says.

Protecting their surroundings (and carbon neutrality) is the hotel's top priority and is achieved through multiple sustainability measures. Everything is heated with wood, including the outdoor pools. The property has six spas—three allow children and three do not, so you can find where you belong. Children are

ALTERNATE STAY

In 2017, Dietmar Mueller-Elmau opened the Orania in Berlin, an urban retreat with reasonable rates in the city's Kreuzberg neighborhood. He calls it the "first wellness hotel without a spa." Taking a page from its sister property, Schloss Elmau, the Orania has regular concerts and events curated by a local jazz pianist.

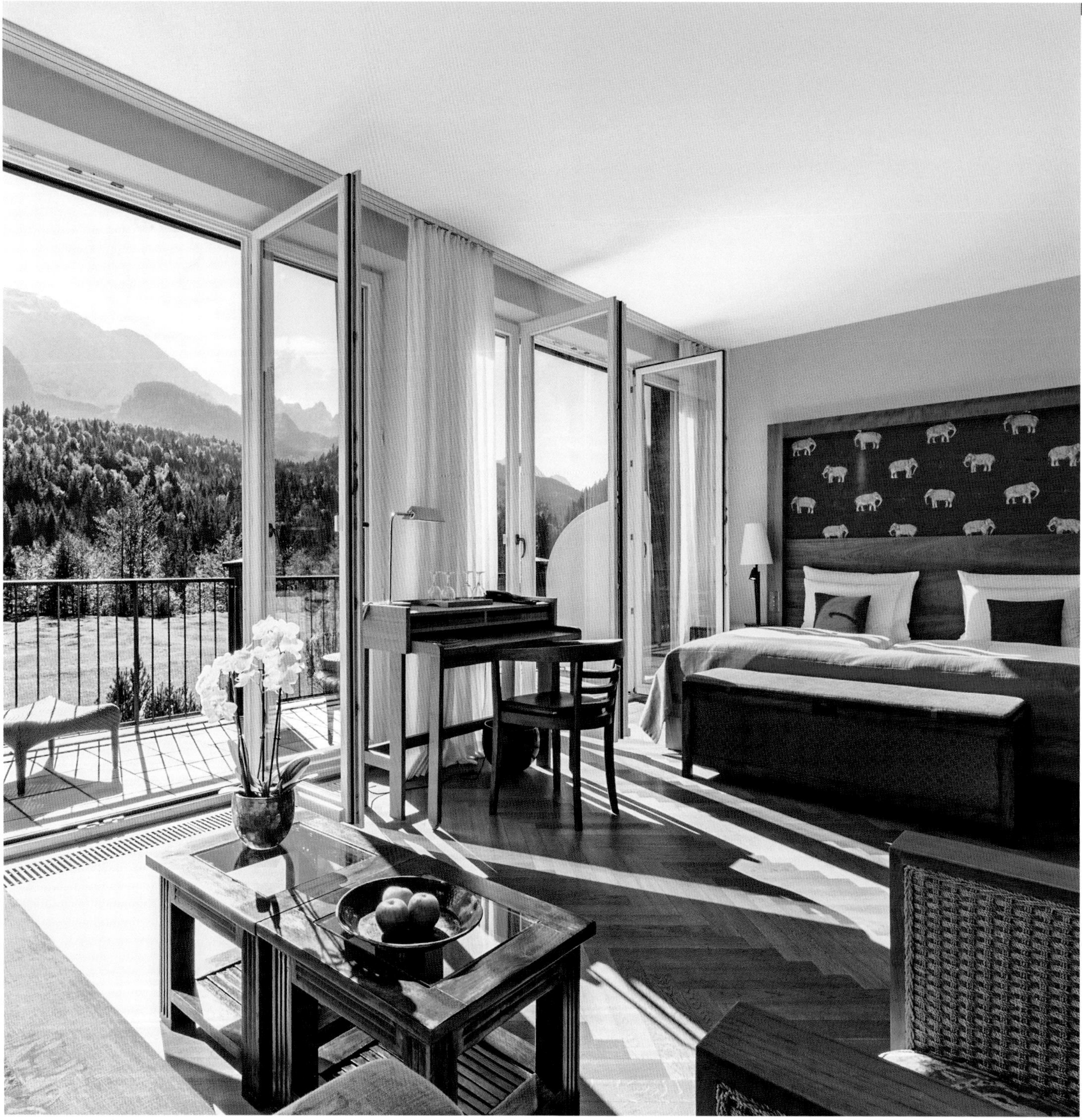

ABOVE: Venture into the natural landscapes of Bavaria, a haven for outdoor adventurers.

OPPOSITE: Stay in Schloss Elmau's Juniorsuite Deluxe for expansive views of rural Germany from your balcony.

always welcome at the kids' club, where they'll find soccer and sports camps, chess academies, science labs, art projects, and much more.

Among the other hotel highlights are the free use of electric BMWs to drive to the fairy-tale castles of King Ludwig, most within an hour of the resort, and the extremely popular e-bikes, of which around 150 are available on-site. The food is varied and high-quality, with several outposts from which to choose, including Japanese, Italian, Thai, and Indian options.

Even with the substantial lineup of offerings, guests still comment most of all on the quality of the staff. They have no formal dress code and are trained to "just be nice and be yourself." A motto for anyone to take with them after checkout.

BERLIN, GERMANY

HOTEL AM STEINPLATZ

Find elegance and comfort tucked away in one of Berlin's residential neighborhoods.

YEAR ESTABLISHED: 1913 **NUMBER OF ROOMS:** 87 **FAMOUS FEATURE:** Inviting courtyard
WHEN TO GO: May–September

As you map out a visit to Berlin, it is helpful to look at the city as a collection of boroughs. Berlin's neighborhoods are massive, built and rebuilt over decades of complex history. One of the best areas to stay in this bustling metropolis is leafy, residential Charlottenburg, home to the Hotel am Steinplatz, Autograph Collection, a wonderfully restored art nouveau masterpiece that first opened in 1913 and has a history of attracting literary and movie stars, including Brigitte Bardot.

Designed by the architect of Berlin's much-visited Hackesche Höfe complex, the light green and off-white facade of the hotel is particularly striking. In summer, the hotel's own courtyard is an inviting place to enjoy local dining specialties and drinks. Rooms are elegant, neutral, and comfortable—never over-the-top. And it has a spacious rooftop spa.

The hotel is within walking distance of the Tiergarten and Kurfürstendamm, a shopping street famous for department store KaDeWe. Because Charlottenburg is so large, it takes about 30 minutes to walk to another beautiful area, the Lietzensee, or the shop- and café-lined Leonhardtstrasse.

The Hotel am Steinplatz allows you to live like a Berliner for a few days in one of the city's most appealing neighborhoods. For grander options, look at the Hotel de Rome, SO/ Berlin Das Stue, and the Hotel Adlon Kempinski (also known as the place where Michael Jackson dangled a baby outside the window).

AFTER CHECK-IN

Many German baking traditions date back centuries. Luisa Weiss, a longtime Berliner, includes many classics in her best-selling cookbook, *Classic German Baking,* in which she also recommends Hutzelmann in Charlottenburg, an independent bakery (and a bit of a time warp), for *streuselkuchen* (crumb cake) and more.

OPPOSITE: With its unique architectural elements, the facade of Hotel am Steinplatz stands out from the other buildings in Berlin's Charlottenburg.

am Steinplatz
HOTEL A

VIENNA, AUSTRIA

HOTEL SACHER

A delicious cake of chocolate and apricot jam put this hotel on the map.

YEAR ESTABLISHED: **1876** NUMBER OF ROOMS: **152** FAMOUS FEATURE: **Original Sacher-Torte**
WHEN TO GO: **April–May or September–October**

In Vienna, the city's most celebrated hotel was built on the fame of a cake. Across all of Austria, the coffee and cake ritual *(kaffee und kuchen)* is irresistible. But the most iconic—and historic—way to partake is at Café Sacher, home to the Original Sacher-Torte, a velvety and light chocolate cake made with a thin layer of apricot jam and a rich, glossy chocolate glaze. Ideally, the cake is served *mit schlag* (with a generous dollop of unsweetened whipped cream), plus your choice of coffee, such as *sacher melange*, which is similar to a cappuccino but with a whipped cream topping.

Today, Hotel Sacher sells 360,000 handmade cakes every year. Throughout the year, one employee cracks up to 9,000 eggs a day to make the cake, but during Christmas season, two people are employed to crack between 16,000 and 18,000 eggs a day.

The Original Sacher-Torte was invented in 1832 by 16-year-old Franz Sacher. The cake immediately became a sensation and was even beloved by Empress Sisi, who famously obsessed over her figure. The recipe is a closely guarded secret that is still used today. In 1876, Franz's son, Eduard, opened the luxurious Hotel Sacher overlooking the Vienna State Opera.

Though anyone can line up for coffee and cake at Café Sacher—and the lines do get long—a stay at the family-run Hotel Sacher is the most glamorous trip back to 19th-century European high society, complemented by modern conveniences and impeccable service, of course. The hotel is located inside the Ringstrasse (Ring Road) that encircles the center of Vienna. The best rooms have views of the opera house or the Albertina museum, which houses one of

OPPOSITE: Try the Original Sacher-Torte, the famous Viennese chocolate cake, at Café Sacher.

PAGES 124–125: Top-floor views, a king-size bed, and multiple seating areas make the Grand Signature Suite a premier room at Hotel Sacher.

ORIGINAL
SACHER
TORTE

the world's largest graphic art collections by masters such as Dürer, Rembrandt, and Rubens in an 18th-century palace. The hotel is also adjacent to the shopping streets that lead to St. Stephen's Cathedral and the Hofburg palace complex.

The hotel's public spaces have kept their Old World charm, but the rooms have been modernized for an airy and elegant feel. The Blaue (Blue) Bar is a richly decorated blue-and-gold hideaway; the Restaurant Rote (Red) Bar is the place to try classic Viennese specialties like the Sacher *tafelspitz* (boiled beef in broth) or Wiener schnitzel.

But it all comes back to the cake—and chocolate. In the spa, guests can choose one of the chocolate treatments, which incorporate elements of the cacao bean. Upon checking into the hotel, each guest receives an Original Sacher-Würfel (or Sacher Cube), and each night at turndown, guests receive another delicious surprise, guaranteeing the sweetest of dreams and a continuous link to the hotel's history.

If you can't make it to Austria, you can order the Original Sacher-Torte to be shipped to your home anywhere in the world.

DRINK IT UP

Located a 15-minute walk from Hotel Sacher, Cafe Sperl is the classic Viennese coffeehouse you picture—a cultural time capsule with shared newspapers mounted on wooden sticks and people ordering multiple coffees. The interior, with golden walls, dark wood panels, and chandeliers, is nearly unchanged from when it opened in 1880.

AMSTERDAM, NETHERLANDS

AMBASSADE HOTEL

With its literary history, this canal house offers a warm and cozy intellectual stay.

YEAR ESTABLISHED: **1953** NUMBER OF ROOMS: **55** FAMOUS FEATURE: **Book events**
WHEN TO GO: **Year-round**

Like many European cities in peak season, Amsterdam suffers from overtourism. But in the slower season, the magic of misty mornings on canals lined with 17th-century homes reveals itself quickly.

The independently owned 55-room Ambassade Hotel is set in 10 historic canal houses (the first one was converted in 1953) in the middle of the "Nine Streets" area, which is conveniently packed with shops and cafés. What makes this hotel one of a kind are its close links to book publishing. At times, it turns into a European literary salon with intimate reading events and author signings. It is a long-running tradition that authors stay here when a Dutch translation of their books is launched. The hotel's collection has more than 5,000 signed books from authors who have stayed here, many lining the walls of the Library Bar.

Owner Wouter Schopman is a publisher himself, but he is also obsessed with CoBrA avant-garde art, a brief but exuberant movement started in 1948 in Paris. More than 800 pieces of art are on display throughout the hotel, including in the light-filled second-floor brasserie overlooking the canal.

This is a warm and intellectual stay, surrounded by books and cozy nooks with blue velvet couches perfect for reading. There are always pots of fresh flowers and a truly exceptional staff. You can also book the hotel's private guide for a biking or walking tour of the city.

AFTER CHECK-IN

Out of central Amsterdam and past the old Olympic Stadium is the Amsterdam Forest, with a magical and funny goat farm, Geitenboerderij Ridammerhoeve. For local kids, this is a beloved tradition where you can feed the goats with baby bottles and eat food made from fresh goat cheese.

OPPOSITE: Ambassade Hotel, an enchanting hotel on one of Amsterdam's famous canals, is illuminated in the early evening.

AMBASSADE HOTEL

MARBELLA, SPAIN

MARBELLA CLUB HOTEL

This family-owned icon on the Spanish coast is known for exquisite gardens and outdoor recreation.

YEAR ESTABLISHED: **1954** NUMBER OF ROOMS: **130** FAMOUS FEATURE: **Kids' club**
WHEN TO GO: **May–September**

In the 1950s, the formerly sleepy village of Marbella in Spain's Andalusia region was put on the map. The story goes that Prince Alfonso of Hohenlohe, whose family was exiled to Madrid, drove his Rolls-Royce to Marbella for a picnic. He fell in love with the area and convinced his family to buy what was then Finca Santa Margarita, thinking it would be a holiday home. The first 20 bedrooms opened to outside guests in 1954.

It was never an actual club, but more a feeling that those who knew about it had found something special. Soon, big names arrived (Brigitte Bardot, Audrey Hepburn) after Alfonso spent time in California studying and making social connections. He also began sneaking seeds back in his suitcase, which would result in a lush Pacific vibe mixed with the local fig and olive trees lining the property.

The 130-room hotel, renamed the Marbella Club in the 1970s, is laid out like a whitewashed Andalusian village, staying true to Prince Alfonso's original edict that none of the buildings would go above the treetops. The style is a sunny meld of Spanish, Californian, and Mexican influences (among the villa names: Casabel and Bel Air), and the decor is a mix of ceramics, bamboo, teak, and whitewashed stone.

Two restaurants remain huge draws for both outside guests and those staying the night. The Grill, fragrant and romantic in candlelight, has been open

OPPOSITE: The Marbella Club's El Patio serves Mediterranean cuisine all day in a finely decorated courtyard.

PAGES 130–131: Walk out on the Marbella Club's dock, extending from the Beach Club on the shore into the Mediterranean's azure waters.

GRANDES FESTEJOS
HERMOSAS PLAYAS
DE
SANLUCAR DE BARRAMEDA

MARBELLA CLUB

nearly as long as the hotel itself. Meanwhile, the mint green and coral Beach Club has a *palapa* roof reminiscent of 1950s Acapulco, where Alfonso loved to visit. The spa offers a range of wellness programs and a regional, health-focused menu.

Alfonso's cousin, Count Rudi, who studied hospitality in Lausanne, was brought on to run the hotel from the start and became its most iconic personality and leader, an integral part of the hotel for decades. The ownership has since passed to the Shamoon family, who grew up going to the Marbella Club. Jennica Shamoon Arazi spearheaded the conversion of the original Hohenlohe family home into one of Europe's best kids' clubs, which has a rolling calendar of activities for kids four and older. Activities include cooking and aromatherapy classes, botanist workshops, art projects, pajama parties, and more.

Marbella is about the good life and outdoor pursuits—tennis and paddle courts, horseback riding on La Concha Mountain, biking, and long walks are always on offer. Within a couple hours' drive are Seville, Granada, Córdoba, and Ronda, which boasts one of Andalusia's top wine scenes.

AFTER CHECK-IN

Most people fly into Málaga, which has become a cultural epicenter for Andalusia. Guests of the Marbella Club often plan a day trip to explore the city's offerings, including the Picasso Museum, the Contemporary Art Centre, and the Soho Theater, owned by Antonio Banderas, who grew up here.

SEVILLE, SPAIN

HOTEL ALFONSO XIII

You'll feel absolutely presidential during a stay at this city treasure, built to entertain visiting elites from around the world.

YEAR ESTABLISHED: **1928** NUMBER OF ROOMS: **148** FAMOUS FEATURE: **VIP guests** WHEN TO GO: **February–May**

Perhaps our most romantic notions of Spain originate in Seville, the birthplace of flamenco and home to the seductions of Don Juan, tapas, and Spain's largest cathedral. Seville is the most visited city in Andalusia and a charming maze of cobblestoned streets and citrus trees. Plan a visit out of peak season (summer temperatures here can feel oppressive) and base yourself at an opulent time capsule built by—and named for—King Alfonso XIII, who wanted a luxurious hotel for elites visiting for the 1929 World Fair in Barcelona. Now a landmark of the city, the hotel continues to have a VIP guest list. Famous guests have included President Barack Obama, who stayed here when speaking at the World Travel & Tourism Council's Global Summit, and a long list of royals.

The hotel's decor features thousands of colorful tiles, graphic-print rugs, and dramatic lighting fixtures. Breakfast in the colonnaded patio overlooking the central courtyard is the best way to start a day of sightseeing at the city's icons like the Alcázar and the 34-story Giralda tower.

The Spanish siesta is a serious daily ritual, and locals take a break from around 2 p.m. to 5 p.m., which is also the best time to retreat to the hotel to enjoy the palm tree–lined outdoor pool or a drink at the art deco–style bar.

Seville can be easily combined with Andalusia's other top properties, including Marbella Club (page 128) and Finca Cortesin (page 153).

OPPOSITE: With its distinct details and architecture, Hotel Alfonso XIII is an iconic cultural landmark.

HOTEL
ALFONSO XIII
SAN FERNANDO 2

LISBON, PORTUGAL

FOUR SEASONS RITZ LISBON

Work out with a view or dine on regional delicacies during a stay at this regional landmark.

YEAR ESTABLISHED: **1959** NUMBER OF ROOMS: **282** FAMOUS FEATURE: **Rooftop track**
WHEN TO GO: **March–May or September–October**

The Four Seasons Ritz Lisbon was built at the urging of António de Oliveira Salazar, who ruled over Portugal for more than 35 years. Salazar recognized that, unlike Paris and London, Lisbon did not have a grande dame hotel. Soon, the landmark art deco meets 18th-century French masterpiece (the designers visited Paris for inspiration) became a triumphant symbol of what tourism could mean for the city and country. What Lisbon has become since is a creative force with a special soul and flavorful cuisine to rival any other European city.

Perched on one of Lisbon's many hills, the modernist exterior belies the elegant interiors, with views of the rooftops and water beyond. The first thing you notice is the scale of the public spaces, complemented by stunning Portuguese art pieces that you can explore via the hotel's own art app. Nearly all the 282 rooms have a terrace, and all have bold, smooth, and elegant finishings, characteristic of art deco but completely modern in feel.

Among the hotel's highlights are the top-floor gym facilities, which include a rooftop running track with city views (look for the original hotel sign, THE RITZ, which you can see from afar in the city). It also has innovative fine dining experiences and a bar with soft velvet seats. The breakfast buffet is one of the best in Europe; savor Portuguese specialties like *pastéis de nata,* custard tarts.

MEET UP

From the hotel, walk via Rua Nova de São Mamede to the bustling main street of the Príncipe Real neighborhood, Rua da Escola Politécnica. Then walk down Rua de São Marçal to Praça das Flores. This charming square is a favorite of Celia Pedroso, co-author of *Eat Portugal,* who brings the city to life through amazing guided food tours. Book with her for a delicious experience—and a new friend in Lisbon.

OPPOSITE: Sprint or jog above the city on the rooftop running track at the Four Seasons Ritz Lisbon.

ATHENS, GREECE

HOTEL GRANDE BRETAGNE

This grand hotel's impressive history and stature could win Olympic gold.

YEAR ESTABLISHED: **1874** NUMBER OF ROOMS: **320** FAMOUS FEATURE: **Suites**
WHEN TO GO: **March–May or September–October**

In Athens, a wonderfully chaotic and heady city, ancient history reigns over the urban sprawl. The Acropolis is never far from sight, and modern parks have been built alongside millennia-old ruins.

By comparison, the Hotel Grande Bretagne—overlooking the Parliament and National Gardens—is comparatively new. Built in the late 1800s as one of the grand neoclassical mansions that once lined the streets of Athens (most have been torn down), the hotel is a designated landmark, and the name cannot be changed. Its guest list has included the hosts of the first modern Olympic Games, held at the nearby all-marble Panathenaic Stadium in 1896.

Through a revolving door and into a double-height lobby, Corinthian columns and symbolic Greek tiles add local flair to the Old World feel of the hotel. The Winter Garden, with an original stained glass ceiling and palm trees, serves afternoon tea; Alexander's Lounge is named for the bar's 18th-century tapestry of Alexander the Great.

Two of the most spectacular hotel suites in the world are here: the Presidential and the silk-lined Royal Suites, with treasures like glasses from the wedding of the last king and queen of Greece on display. The head butler gives weekly historical tours of the suites to guests.

Dine at the rooftop restaurant, which boasts the only-in-Athens view of the Acropolis. Breakfast is for guests only, but anyone can book lunch or dinner.

MEET UP

Book Angelos Kokkaliaris *(athens walkingguide.com)* for an in-depth (and humorous) tour of the city. Walk 10 minutes from the hotel to the leafy hillside Kolonaki neighborhood. Visit the Museum of Cycladic Art, and enjoy coffee and people-watching at Péros café.

OPPOSITE: GB Roof Garden Restaurant & Bar offers unobstructed views of ancient Greek buildings, including the Acropolis.

SANTORINI, GREECE

CANAVES COLLECTION

This family-owned hotel collection offers respite from the island crowds with a range of options—and views.

YEAR ESTABLISHED: 1983 **NUMBER OF ROOMS:** Varies by location **FAMOUS FEATURE:** Historic caves
WHEN TO GO: May–October

Yes, Greece has other, less crowded islands worth visiting. But Santorini is mythic on another level—a mighty volcanic eruption nearly 4,000 years ago created one of the world's most legendary views when part of the original island fell into the sea, leaving the caldera, or volcanic crater, behind. From a catamaran tour, you'll think the village of Oia (arguably the island's prettiest) looks like a dusting of powdered sugar on top of a dark cliff sloping to the sea.

Santorini's visitor numbers have gone from almost nonexistent in the 1950s to sometimes overwhelming. The Chaidemenos family, who runs the Canaves Collection, has helped shape tourism here, from the airy all-white aesthetic to high-quality dining and insider access to local experiences.

It all began when managing director Markos Chaidemenos's father inherited three *canaves* (caves), structures historically used to store wine at stable temperatures throughout the year. Originally, the famous part of the island wasn't the cliffside; the richest inhabitants were wine producers in the flatlands. As tourism evolved, the cliff became the place to be, and in 1983 the Chaidemenos family turned the inherited caves into a hotel that is today called **Canaves Ena.** The family also owns a few properties on Santorini and is expanding to other Greek islands.

OPPOSITE: Soak up the sun by the pool the Santorini way, with panoramas of the Mediterranean and other Greek islands.

PAGES 140–141: On Petra Restaurant & Bar's Panorama Balcony, guests eat fine Greek cuisine and watch the sun set over the Santorini caldera.

Pool Rules

The flagship is **Canaves Oia Suites,** a postcard-perfect dream with the best location at the beginning of the pedestrianized village, a spa built into a historic cave, and a stunning fine dining restaurant next to the pool. The eight-room **Canaves Sunday** is often bought out for multi-generational trips, and if you book one restaurant in Santorini (even if you're not staying the night), make it the top-floor restaurant here, which offers 360-degree views of the island and an unforgettable sunset.

Canaves Epitome is the newest hotel in the Chaidemenos portfolio. After expanding beyond the cliffside, the family took a gamble on the "sunset" part of the island above Amoudi Bay. Here, it is about more space and privacy. Epitome is the only property in the portfolio that allows children.

Book your stay in late April or October, and bring a light scarf. You'll find far fewer crowds, much less expensive hotel rates, and warm sunshine during the day. Nights are mildly cool, the perfect weather for walks and exploring the island's wineries. After dining on local grilled fish and vegetables in Amoudi Bay, hike the uneven 300 steps to Oia to enjoy a cup at Lolita's Gelato.

LOCAL ACCESS

A boat ride in the caldera is a Santorini must-do. The Chaidemenos family turned a passion for the sea into a business with Sunset Oia yachts and catamarans. Book a morning or sunset tour that includes stops for swimming and a delicious Greek barbecue meal.

OTOČEC, SLOVENIA

HOTEL GRAD OTOČEC

A renovated castle offers five-star luxury in an oft overlooked part of the world.

YEAR ESTABLISHED: **1959** NUMBER OF ROOMS: **16** FAMOUS FEATURE: **Wine tasting in a castle tower**
WHEN TO GO: **May–June or September–October**

Slovenia is one of the most wonderful yet underrated destinations in Europe—though the number of visitors is growing significantly each year.

It takes just two and a half hours to drive from Venice, Italy, to the walkable capital of Ljubljana, Slovenia, a cobblestoned city of pastel-colored houses and riverside cafés. Beyond the capital, you'll find incredible natural beauty and a high quality of life. It's also a place where a higher-end trip with top dining, cultural experiences, and five-star hotels costs significantly less than in Europe's other capital cities.

Mattej Valenčič and Matej Knific, the founders of Luxury Slovenia, plan trips across the country's unique blend of Alpine, Mediterranean, and Pannonian landscapes. In little more than an hour, you can journey from the majestic Alps to the serene sea. One of the top hotels on their itineraries is Hotel Grad Otočec, just 45 minutes from Ljubljana. The historic castle was transformed into a getaway within a fairy tale–like setting in Thermal Pannonian Slovenia, known for natural thermal baths with healing properties.

"The endless peace, nature, exquisite cuisine, and service are what convinces us to return time and again," says Valenčič. Slovenia has more than 200 castles, but many of them lie in ruins. "This hotel is the only castle in the middle of a river. More than 60 percent of Slovenia is covered by forests, so it is an especially unique combination where nature merges with a castle experience."

AFTER CHECK-IN

Many trips planned by Luxury Slovenia include a visit to the nearby monastery in Kostanjevica, which is also home to the Božidar Jakac Art Museum, where you can enjoy a superb collection of artwork, attend a concert, or create your own art print. For those with an adventurous spirit, row around the small island of Kostanjevica na Krki to immerse yourself in nature near Otočec Castle.

OPPOSITE: Hotel Grad Otočec, located on an islet in the Krka River, is surrounded by the Slovenian countryside.

ABOVE: The Superior Suite, the most spacious of the hotel's bedrooms, features earth-toned furnishings and natural materials.

OPPOSITE: A fly fisherman casts his line into the Krka River in hopes of catching Danube salmon or trout.

It's a castle stay without the slightly musty atmosphere. Guests will find a place for local wine tastings in one of the towers; an 18-hole golf course; and an organic garden that supplies the castle's award-winning restaurant, which focuses on Slovenian specialties (anyone can book a table, regardless of spending the night).

The country's cuisine is heavily influenced by neighboring cultures, especially Austria and Hungary (it was part of the Austro-Hungarian Empire for centuries), but also Italy and the Balkans. A jar of honey is the must-have souvenir—there are more beekeepers per capita than anywhere in the world. The beekeeping tradition here has been recognized by UNESCO as an intangible cultural heritage. And after years of efforts by the Slovenian government, the United Nations declared May 20 as World Bee Day.

ISTANBUL, TURKEY

ÇIRAĞAN PALACE KEMPINSKI

A 19th-century palace keeps its Old World charm and provides delights for all senses.

YEAR ESTABLISHED: **1991** NUMBER OF ROOMS: **317** FAMOUS FEATURE: **Views of the Bosporus**
WHEN TO GO: **April–May or September–October**

The Çırağan Palace is a glorious historic hotel that could only be in Istanbul, where East meets West and Asia meets Europe. The city is a geographical and cultural crossroads. Visit here and all the senses light up from seeing the dramatic tiles of the Blue Mosque or browsing in the teeming Grand Bazaar, with more than 4,000 shops and the intoxicating scents of Turkish coffee, dates and apricots, leather, tobacco, and spices.

The palace is the former residence of Sultan Abdülaziz, the 32nd sultan of the Ottoman Empire, which lasted for six centuries. The Old World feel of the palace, finished in 1867 and opened to guests in 1991, is overwhelmingly nostalgic and beautiful, set against the backdrop of the Bosporus.

Each day should begin by gazing at the river, its significance as a strategic trade route not lost on you as a parade of shipping containers, ferries, private yachts, and Turkish *gulets* (two- or three-masted sailboats) pass by. After breakfast on the terrace and a day of sightseeing, return to admire the colorful handmade Turkish rugs in the lobby, swim in the infinity pool that seems to drop into the Bosporus, dive into hammam culture at the spa, or enjoy Turkish-Mediterranean food.

The hotel has 11 suites, the most elegant being the Haseki Sultan Suite. The newer Pasha Suite has its own hammam, steam room, and three balconies; it's also serviced by a 24-hour butler.

MEET UP

Karen Fedorko Sefer, a former fashion executive, runs one of the top tour companies in Turkey: Sea Song Tours. Whether you want a private gulet voyage, a Turkish carpet, the best restaurant recommendations, or a resort vacation on the Aegean coast, Fedorko Sefer has unmatched connections and knowledge.

OPPOSITE: The splendid grounds of Çırağan Palace Kempinski, the only palace and five-star luxury hotel found on the Bosporus

HELLA, ICELAND

HESTHEIMAR GUESTHOUSE

A cozy guesthouse and horse farm sets the scene for true Icelandic hospitality.

YEAR ESTABLISHED: **2007** NUMBER OF ROOMS: **16** FAMOUS FEATURE: **Horses**
WHEN TO VISIT: **June–March**

On average, Iceland has seven to eight times more tourists than locals. Super-luxe hotels, such as Deplar Farm and the Retreat at the Blue Lagoon, have been built to appeal to discerning travelers.

But to experience the *real* Iceland, try the charming Hestheimar guesthouse, set on a horse farm and run by a local couple who live here with their three children. A main house and six cozy guest cottages are scattered throughout the property, all powered by geothermal energy. The views are astounding: not just of the sprawling ranch, but also of the Hekla and Eyjafjallajökull volcanoes. Rooms are named after horses on the farm, and you can wander around to meet them—if they don't make a point to meet you first; don't worry, they're friendly—or take riding lessons. Hestheimar is located just an hour from Reykjavík. Not too far off the Golden Circle, it makes for an ideal launching point to see Iceland's highlights.

"What I love about it is they make homemade meals, like lasagna, fresh bread, and traditional lamb stew," says Lauren Bryan Knight, founder of Open Invite Trips, who has visited Iceland more than 15 times. Your stay at Hestheimar includes breakfast, and during summer months and Christmastime it also includes lunch and dinner. "There is always coffee and cake. It's not fancy, but it's comfortable and it's the Iceland you go for, the perfect example of Icelandic hospitality. When I recommend it to people, I get an email back at the end of their trip, saying, 'We had the best time there and it was so cozy.'"

OPPOSITE: **Hestheimar guesthouse's Icelandic horses trot through freshly fallen snow.**

EUROPE

BONUS STAYS

CROATIA

Hotel Excelsior, ***Dubrovnik***

Hotel Excelsior is the historic grande dame of Dubrovnik. Now owned by Adriatic Luxury Hotels, it occupies a prime seaside locale in the "Pearl of the Adriatic," just a 10-minute walk from the Old City. Among the many celebrated former guests are Queen Elizabeth II (with Prince Philip and Princess Anne in 1972) and Elizabeth Taylor.

IRELAND

Adare Manor, ***Adare***

Close to the charming village of Adare, Adare Manor was renovated top to bottom in 2017 and is now one of the best hotels in Ireland. Among the outdoor activities to immerse yourself into the Irish countryside are falconry, clay pigeon shooting, biking, archery, golf, and more. Plus, it has a fantastic spa to wind down.

The Westbury, ***Dublin***

Perhaps the best located hotel in Dublin—just off Grafton Street, the main shopping corridor—the Westbury is part of the Irish-owned Doyle Collection. The dining spaces are beautiful, especially the Gallery for afternoon tea. Relax with a coffee by the fireplace in the expansive second-floor lobby before walking to any number of close-by attractions, like St. Stephen's Green or Trinity College and the Book of Kells.

ITALY

Borgo Egnazia, ***Savelletri***

Owned by the wonderful Aldo Melpignano, Borgo Egnazia was created to mimic a traditional Puglian village near the coast. The result is a magical, whitewashed Italian paradise lit by thousands of (fake) candles. It's perfect for families: The hotel offers both kids' and teens' clubs and events like cooking demonstrations and alfresco parties set in the central piazza.

Grand Hotel Majestic già Baglioni, ***Bologna***

The grande dame of Bologna has faced the city's main cathedral since 1911. And as expected, the interiors of this 106-room property are grand, reminiscent of an Italian palazzo—marble floors, antique furniture, and rich fabrics. Book a fourth-floor junior suite for a private balcony that overlooks the city, or the Art Deco Terrace Suite for the ultimate stay.

Punta Tragara, ***Capri***

A stylish icon designed by Le Corbusier in 1920, the apricot-colored,

OPPOSITE: Borgo Egnazia in Italy offers dinner and an inspiring show—Pizzica dancing, a nod to traditional village festivals.

PAGES 152–153: Park Hotel Vitznau, an opulent Swiss retreat, is located on the tranquil shores of Lake Lucerne.

family-owned Punta Tragara on Capri feels a world away from the madness of the oft crowded island. The hotel is a bastion of art deco elegance with glamorous stories to tell and overlooks the bright blue Mediterranean and famous Faraglioni rocks.

SPAIN

Finca Cortesin, *Casares*

The hacienda-style Finca Cortesin is the perfect base from which to explore Andalusia's whitewashed villages. Its four pools (one at the fabulous Mediterranean Beach Club), an impressive spa, and indoor/outdoor dining on twinkly-lit patios make a wonderfully serene southern Spain setting. (Combine with a stay at nearby Marbella Club, page 128.)

SWITZERLAND

Alex Lake Zürich, *Thalwil*

Located just 20 minutes by train from Zurich's city center, the hotel, in the posh village of Thalwil, feels like a local secret. Residents fill the outdoor bar and terrace alongside hotel guests to partake in the excellent food every evening. Designed by Campbell Gray, the best rooms have private terraces where guests can enjoy their morning coffee overlooking the lake, before jumping in for some wild swimming. Like the Widder in central Zurich (page 92), the Alex is part of the Living Circle hotel group.

Castello del Sole, *Ascona*

This magical retreat with lush gardens on the shores of Lake Maggiore is a

ABOVE: In Spain, opt for a game of golf at Finca Cortesin's stunning course.

OPPOSITE: Start the day with breakfast on the balcony of the deluxe master room at Punta Tragara on Capri, Italy.

PAGES 156–157: The Presidential Suite of the Grand Hotel Majestic già Baglioni in Bologna, Italy

10-minute bike ride from Ascona. The hotel's style evokes the luxurious ranches of the western U.S. or Argentina, with earthy yellows and pinks (except for the bar, which is outfitted with marine blue tiles and orange lamps), arched windows, and extensive alfresco seating. (Combine a stay here with one at Hotel Eden Roc Ascona, page 86.)

Dolder Grand, *Zurich*

The Dolder Grand—which looks like a Swiss castle on a hill—first opened in 1899 and has evolved to become the ultimate urban retreat. Just 15 minutes from Zurich, it offers panoramic views over the city and lake. With a museum-quality art collection, a popular Sunday brunch, and a wonderful spa, the Dolder is a welcome addition to any Switzerland itinerary.

Park Hotel Vitznau, *Vitznau*

The best arrival to the Park Hotel Vitznau is by boat from Lucerne, about an hour away. Pulling up to the hotel by boat is

absolutely dreamy. Though the exterior looks like a castle, with its pointed turrets, the interior is all futuristic, with sleek lines and contemporary furniture. Amenities include fine dining options with almost all products sourced from the region, a cutting-edge health and wellness clinic, and an indoor/outdoor pool. Vitznau is the jumping-off point for an excursion to the top of Mount Rigi. In 1871, the first mountain railway in Europe took tourists to the peak.

UNITED KINGDOM

Firmdale Hotels, *London, England*

The distinctly colorful and textured aesthetic at London's Firmdale Hotels—led by co-founder and designer Kit Kemp—has become synonymous with a very specific whimsical British style. Among the top properties in London are the Covent Garden Hotel, the Ham Yard Hotel, and the Haymarket Hotel. All have buzzy dining outlets that are equally as appealing for local Londoners as they are for visitors.

Star Castle Hotel, *Isles of Scilly, England*

Located 28 miles (45 km) off the coast of Cornwall, England, the Isles of Scilly are a quintessential holiday spot, lesser known by foreigners because they are not quick or easy to get to from London (out of 140 islands, only five are inhabited). Star Castle Hotel was built in the shape of an eight-pointed star in 1593 for defense purposes; today it is a lovely family-owned and -operated getaway. Book a garden suite for a cozy English cottage feel.

PART TWO

NORTH AMERICA & THE CARIBBEAN

Swim above the clouds in the luxurious infinity pool at Big Sur's Post Ranch Inn (page 160).

BIG SUR, CALIFORNIA, U.S.A.

POST RANCH INN

A trendsetter in sustainability, this cliffside stay offers dramatic views and a chance to unplug.

YEAR ESTABLISHED: **1992** NUMBER OF ROOMS: **40** FAMOUS FEATURE: **Sierra Mar restaurant**
WHEN TO GO: **April–November**

In 1982, Mike Freed purchased a plot of land in Big Sur, California, from Billy Post, whose grandfather homesteaded the property in the 1860s. Captured by the area's magic, Freed built a cabin in an enclave on the central California coast that became one of the first solar houses in the state.

Ten years later, he and Billy Post, now Freed's business partner, opened the Post Ranch Inn. The stunning property would become an industry-leading model for sustainable luxury.

In 1992, having any sort of sustainability program at a hotel was highly unusual. As Freed says, "We try to set examples—we don't expect everyone to do what we do, but everyone can do better, including us." Today, Post Ranch Inn is powered from renewable resources, including wind, solar, and geothermal. Freed is a solar power enthusiast and installed 990 panels in 2009 (the most at a hotel at the time), which has reduced carbon emissions significantly. Almost everything served or provided at the inn is an organic product: fruit, vegetables, cotton sheets (made in California without dyes or chemicals), mattresses (handmade one at a time by a local artisan), and even spa products.

At 1,200 feet (366 m) in elevation, the inn sits in a pocket that Freed says has the "clearest atmospheric condition in our hemisphere, with no air or light pollution." When they planned to develop it, "the whole idea was to not impose on the landscape," he says. "After we hired [Big Sur architect] Mickey Muennig, he went to every location where rooms would go and slept in a sleeping bag. We wanted to do three things: create ultimate privacy; capture

OPPOSITE: A young buck grazes on the grounds of the sustainability-conscious Post Ranch Inn, much of which is maintained as a protected area.

PAGES 162–163: On the upper deck of the Pacific Suite, you can find sweeping views of the rugged Big Sur coastline.

the views (the mountain views are as spectacular as the ocean); and not disturb the landscape."

Some rooms are stand-alone ocean-view houses; others are built with natural grasses on top. The redwood paneling throughout is a Post Ranch signature–half is reclaimed wood; half came from old, remilled wine vats. The inn has no televisions—though you'll find great sound systems for music—and guests are grateful for the forced disconnect.

The inn's restaurant, Sierra Mar is arguably one of the most beautiful places to dine in the entire world. The food and wine focus on the region's abundance. Watch for the endangered California condors soaring outside the restaurant from its floor-to-ceiling windows. "The coolest thing is seeing the condors above and the whales below," says Freed.

Included in the (yes, high) room rate is breakfast, the minibar, and a slate of complimentary activities, including guided walks and yoga. The staff are exceptional—some were born on the property and now work for the hotel.

ALTERNATE STAY

As you cross the Golden Gate Bridge from San Francisco to Sausalito, you'll get a glimpse of Cavallo Point (also owned by Mike Freed), a beautiful lodge set on a former military base, Fort Baker. The last soldier left in 2000, and the fort is now managed by the National Park Service. The hotel has unmatched views of the bridge, cozy fireplaces, and the wellness-focused Healing Arts Center & Spa. Kids and dogs are welcome.

LOS ANGELES, CALIFORNIA, U.S.A.

THE BEVERLY HILLS HOTEL

You'll have stars in your eyes at this Hollywood institution, known for hosting the likes of Marilyn Monroe and Frank Sinatra.

YEAR ESTABLISHED: 1912 **NUMBER OF ROOMS:** 223 **FAMOUS FEATURE:** Hollywood glamour **WHEN TO GO:** Year-round

Before Rodeo Drive and two years before the city of Beverly Hills even officially existed, the Beverly Hills Hotel was built in 1912, surrounded by nothing but fields. The "Pink Palace" is owned by the Dorchester Collection now and features more than 200 rooms and 23 bungalows that hold Hollywood secrets. The rooms honor former guests, including Marilyn Monroe (Bungalow 1), Elizabeth Taylor (usually Bungalow 5), and Frank Sinatra (Bungalow 22).

"What really sets this hotel apart from the rest is that it is beloved by locals," says Angeleno Stephanie Steinman. "People choose to come here to celebrate special moments, and that says everything." More than most cities, L.A.'s hotels are living rooms for locals and visitors alike—a spot for power lunches, catching up over salads and mocktails, and sunset views. The Beverly Hills Hotel is one such spot.

The moment you walk in, you feel the Golden Age of Hollywood—and recognize the signature banana leaf wallpaper, first introduced in the 1940s. The Fountain Coffee Room (called "the counter" by those in the know) is a 1950s-style diner that has evolved to serve not only pancakes and apple pie, but also green juices and egg-white omelets—this is L.A., after all. Like all great hotels, the staff makes the place, and the Beverly Hills Hotel Quarter Century Club honors employees who have worked here more than 25 years.

AFTER CHECK-IN

Anyone can book a table for lunch at the Polo Lounge, built in the 1930s, for dining alfresco with palm trees wrapped in twinkly lights and pink flowers everywhere. The chopped McCarthy Salad is an institution, with grilled chicken, cheddar, smoked bacon, beets, egg, avocado, and balsamic vinaigrette.

OPPOSITE: Poolside dining at The Cabana Cafe is part of the true Hollywood experience.

LAKE GEORGE, NEW YORK, U.S.A.

THE SAGAMORE

For long summer days and campfire nights, book a room—or a lodge—at this upstate legacy retreat.

YEAR ESTABLISHED: 1883 **NUMBER OF ROOMS:** 137 **FAMOUS FEATURE:** Terraced gardens
WHEN TO GO: May–September

"Lake George is without comparison the most beautiful water I ever saw," said Thomas Jefferson in 1791 as he toured upstate New York. This is still true today, as strict regulations have kept the lake as unspoiled as it was in Jefferson's time—and the maple and beech trees of the Adirondacks and hundreds of small green islands studded throughout the deep blue water only add to the area's appeal.

The best view of Lake George is, without a doubt, from the colonnaded terrace of The Sagamore Resort, a bright white Colonial Revival triumph, with deep green shutters and Adirondack chairs set out on the terraced gardens.

The Sagamore (meaning "respected chief" in the Indigenous Abenaki language) was first built in 1883 on the private Green Island. The pleasures of an Americana summer are easily found here—long days, lake jumping, lobster rolls, evening air scented with barbecue and firepit smoke. Guests can ride on *The Morgan*, a model of a 19th-century tour boat, or play on one of two tennis courts or the 18-hole golf course just a shuttle ride away. Don't skip on winter visits either; the hotel's large rec center offers loads of indoor entertainment, from mini-golf to a movie theater, to keep everyone busy.

As far as your stay, the rooms in the main building are best, but families often choose the lodge suites (some have kitchens). Nothing is overly ostentatious or luxurious, but there is a great legacy here—and you may join the families who return every year.

QUOTABLE

Summer is peak season here, but fall brings lower rates and leaf peeping. In a hallway dedicated to historic documents, read a letter from T. Edmund Krumbholz to a friend in New York City: "When the magic spell of September days lures you to the open country, you could not think of a more glorious spot than The Sagamore on Lake George."

OPPOSITE: The Sagamore, the premier resort on Lake George

NEW YORK, NEW YORK, U.S.A.

CROSBY STREET HOTEL

Brilliant color, noteworthy art, and all-day dining are hallmarks of what has become a classic New York stay.

YEAR ESTABLISHED: 2009 **NUMBER OF ROOMS: 86** **FAMOUS FEATURE: Brilliant color and artwork**
WHEN TO VISIT: Year-round

Like in all of the world's great cities, choosing one hotel of a lifetime in Manhattan is impossible. This is a city filled with remarkable stays: the Carlyle, the Mark, and the Lowell on the Upper East Side; the Baccarat and the Chatwal in Midtown; the Greenwich downtown; and 1 Brooklyn Bridge (page 237) across the river.

But any great New York City hotel must also be a reflection of its neighborhood, part of the fabric of the city's distinct environs. The Crosby Street Hotel, with its luxurious British whimsy and New York soul, is embedded in SoHo, a place for New Yorkers to meet for a meal as much as it is a jumping-off point for visitors. You can no longer imagine the cobblestoned streets of SoHo without the hotel—and its ideal location puts you within walking distance of the West Village, Tribeca, Nolita, and Chinatown, as well as all the buzz of downtown's restaurants, shopping, and streets.

The duality of community gathering space and beloved place for visitors to stay is a hallmark of Firmdale Hotels, founded by Tim and Kit Kemp. Their properties in London (the Covent Garden Hotel and Haymarket Hotel among them) are now classics. The Crosby Street Hotel was their first property in New York; the Whitby in Midtown opened in 2017, and the Warren Street Hotel in Tribeca opened in 2024.

OPPOSITE: Sip a cup of tea and savor sandwiches and treats during an afternoon tea at the Crosby Street Hotel.

PAGES 170-171: Find an inviting place to rest in the colorful drawing room at the Crosby Street Hotel.

Kit Kemp's brilliant design aesthetic of bright colors and patterns is guaranteed to make you happy. And her eye for quirky, uncommon art is seen throughout the public spaces and rooms. "The hotel has settled into its space like someone settling into a very comfortable armchair," she says, "and in that way it looks like the art is a part of the place, rather than a gallery."

One theme is dogs, seen as paintings and sculptures throughout the hotel—an homage to how much New Yorkers love their pets. As for the rooms, the most impressive options are Meadow Suites, with their own peaceful garden terraces, or the sophisticated Crosby Suites. Rooms on higher floors have far-reaching city views (you'll find yourself counting the water towers on the skyline).

The Crosby Bar & Terrace is a true all-day, convivial brasserie with an extensive breakfast and brunch menu, plus lunch and dinner. Afternoon tea is served daily. Seating stretches from the front to the back of the ground floor, with an alfresco terrace for sunny days.

AFTER CHECK-IN

Some of New York's most beloved restaurants are around the corner from the hotel, including renowned institution Balthazar. Don't miss dinner at Raoul's, open since 1975, when SoHo was filled with artists living in cheap lofts. This dimly lit French bistro offers steak au poivre and roast chicken—and incredible people-watching.

VARIOUS LOCATIONS, HAWAII, U.S.A.

FOUR SEASONS HAWAII

Called a "splurge of a lifetime," these island hotels deliver excellent accommodations fit for their beachfront settings.

YEAR ESTABLISHED: **1990 (Maui); 1991 (Lanai); 1996 (Hualalai); 2016 (Oahu)** NUMBER OF ROOMS: **Varies by location**
FAMOUS FEATURE: **Pristine beaches** WHEN TO GO: **Year-round**

"I won't let my clients come to Hawaii without going to the Four Seasons Hualalai," says Stephanie Malakie, founder of Empress Travel Club. "It will always be worth it to stay at the best hotel in the state. My recommendation is to splurge and stay there. Everyone always goes the extra mile."

In fact, all of the Four Seasons properties across the island state are known for pristine beaches and an aloha spirit. With high room rates, these hotels are a splurge of a lifetime—but the experience is so extraordinary that it somehow feels like excellent value.

Among the highlights at **Four Seasons Hualalai** on the Big Island are the two-story bungalows with torchlit paths, multiple swimming pools (including King's Pond, which doubles as an enormous outdoor aquarium), an incredible kids' club with free all-day childcare, the ability to book time with staff marine biologists to feed one of the world's oldest eagle rays, and a swim-up bar where bartenders pluck ingredients from the surrounding garden: Fresh mint for your mojito? They grow it here.

Of the hotel's nearly 250 rooms, Malakie, who lives on the island, most often books guests in the Beach Tree crescent area, where ground-floor rooms have outdoor lava rock showers.

Thirty minutes from Honolulu on Oahu, the **Four Seasons Oahu at Ko Olina**

ALTERNATE STAY

Aulani, A Disney Resort & Spa shares a beach with the Four Seasons Oahu at Ko Olina. It's a childhood dream destination designed to honor Hawaiian and Polynesian traditions. Favorite Disney characters appear throughout the day, and you can snorkel in the resort's private lagoon.

OPPOSITE: Kids of all ages can learn about Hawaiian culture and customs at the Four Seasons in Maui.

PAGES 174–175: Watch a grand sunset from the expansive Ho'onanea Villa at Hualalali resort in Kona.

is set on a beach with calm waters made for stand-up paddleboarding and is well situated for visits to the island's top sites, like Pearl Harbor and the Diamond Head Crater. "You can easily get to the magical North Shore," says Malakie. "Stop at the Dole Plantation along the way for ice cream." A caveat: "This is the only island where I really worry about traffic, so avoid rush hour at all costs."

The **Four Seasons Resort Maui** reigns over Wailea Beach, with other popular hotels nearby (Grand Wailea, Fairmont Kea Lani). The experience begins in the open-air lobby, leading out to a central pool with grand fountains and views to the island of Molokini. This is a celebration resort, with many coming for a honeymoon and returning for family reunions or birthdays. And if it looks familiar—yes, it doubled as the White Lotus hotel for season one of the HBO hit.

You can learn to scuba dive in one of the shallow pools before heading out to the ocean, or book a cabana at the adults-only Serenity Pool. A room with club access offers "one of the best breakfast tables in the resort," says Malakie,

WHILE YOU'RE THERE

Though Waikiki has grown immensely since the Moana Surfrider (now a Westin) opened in 1901, it still feels quintessentially Hawaiian to walk up and down the hotel's oceanfront drive, watching surfers. Other top hotels on Oahu include Halekulani in Waikiki and Turtle Bay on the North Shore. Don't miss the Sunrise Shack for smoothies and acai bowls.

ABOVE: In view of the Wai'nanae Range, the Oahu at Ko Olina resort hugs the rocky coastline.

OPPOSITE: Enjoy the gentle ocean breeze on a luxury catamaran trip off the coast of Lanai.

"a tiny balcony with two tables overlooking the grounds and ocean."

Only one passenger ferry remains in operation in Hawaii, and it runs from Maui to Lanai. The island of Lanai—often called Hawaii's "last unspoiled island"—is now about 98 percent owned by billionaire Larry Ellison, who also owns the **Four Seasons Resort Lanai** and **Sensei Lanai, A Four Seasons Resort.** "Walking around the grounds is part of the experience," Malakie says. "It's quiet and somehow unreal." At Sensei, which focuses on personalized wellness itineraries, there are "surprisingly lower rates, but you pay for the spa treatments, so buy it as a package for a better deal."

An added bonus to your stay: All of the Four Seasons properties in Hawaii have measurable sustainability practices, including water-use reduction, biodiversity, and conservation, and support the local community.

ORLANDO, FLORIDA, U.S.A.

DISNEY'S ANIMAL KINGDOM LODGE

Giraffes and zebras graze outside your window in a Serengeti-inspired hotel that delivers Disney magic.

YEAR ESTABLISHED: **2001** NUMBER OF ROOMS: **1,293** FAMOUS FEATURE: **Safari animals on property**
WHEN TO GO: **Year-round**

Disney's Animal Kingdom Lodge presents its own interpretation of an African safari experience, proving that only in Disney is anything possible. The magic here is real. Yes, it's "safari light," but you get a sense of what a real safari in the Serengeti might be like. And here, children of all ages are welcomed like a (lion) king.

"When I wake up in the morning and walk out onto my hotel balcony, I see a view like no other of giraffes and zebras," says Jeffrey Merola, owner of Mouse Vacation Planning and Storybook Vacation Planning. "I am amazed whenever I walk into the spectacular lobby."

The brainchild of Disney Imagineer Joe Rohde, the hotel's six-story lobby is a soaring welcome to the Animal Kingdom Lodge and is filled with African crafts, artwork, and furnishings. The design is based on a variety of African safari lodges, but a lobby like this is American in scale—aka BIG. Also big is the lodge itself, which is divided into two main buildings—Jambo House (the original hotel and where the lobby is) and Kidani Village, which also has Disney Vacation Club villas. The best rooms have club-level service with all-day food and drink access and cast members to help plan out your itinerary.

The pools, with two long waterslides, are oases even in the heat of Florida summer. And at Jambo House, there's a flamingo pond and playground right by the pool, and every other night s'mores are on offer by the firepit. The

OPPOSITE: A giraffe poses for the camera outside Disney's Animal Kingdom Lodge.

PAGES 180–181: The grand lobby of Disney's Animal Kingdom Lodge boasts authentic artifacts, thatched ceilings, and a mud fireplace.

area also has plenty by way of shopping and food offerings, too: Mombasa Marketplace sells handmade and unique African imports, including toys and clothing. For dining, Jiko restaurant is inspired by many African cultures, Boma has massive buffet options, and Sanaa serves up Indian-inspired food (don't miss ordering the bread service).

Significant effort has been put into every design element, food choice, and interaction to highlight and, therefore, hopefully teach about a wide variety of African cultures through drumming, cultural guides, parties, culinary tours, and more. Even if you're not staying here, you can book a one-hour Starlight Safari for savanna viewing on the lodge grounds.

You will, of course, spend time at Disney's Animal Kingdom Theme Park, with the now iconic Tree of Life at its center. Guests also have easy access to the other Walt Disney World parks and Disney Springs via a free shuttle service. And returning to your home on the savanna, with more than 200 animals, makes a Disney visit extra special.

ALTERNATE STAY

Disney's Grand Floridian Resort & Spa is a dream stay close to the Magic Kingdom Theme Park at Walt Disney World. The holiday season is particularly magical, says Jeffrey Merola, with a full-size gingerbread house in the lobby. "There are wonderful dining experiences like Narcoossee's, Cítricos, and Victoria & Albert's," he says. "You can even walk to the Magic Kingdom from the hotel."

SARATOGA, WYOMING, U.S.A.

BRUSH CREEK RANCH

From horseback riding to culinary excellence, this dude ranch offers a high-end version of the American West.

YEAR ESTABLISHED: **2008** NUMBER OF ROOMS: **69** FAMOUS FEATURE: **Goat yoga** WHEN TO GO: **June–November**

All-inclusive is taken to another level at Brush Creek Ranch, where you'll fall in love with the spirit of the American West. This quintessential yet luxury dude ranch is set on 30,000 acres (12,140 ha) in southern Wyoming, close to the Colorado border.

Beyond the usual outdoor pursuits are offerings such as llama hikes, barrel racing, cattle drives, cheesemaking, pastry classes, and more. Here, goats are superstars, and the cutest options to interact with them include goat yoga and bottle-feeding kids. With its 2-to-1 staff-to-guest ratio, all your Western wishes are catered to, including unparalleled horseback riding.

Almost all activities are included in the rate of your stay, as are three gourmet farm-to-table meals daily. The summer Creekside Dinner Camp is a must, and don't miss the classic Saloon, with cocktails and pool.

The land was purchased from the original homesteader family by the late Bruce White, a longtime hotelier. Originally meant to be his family's personal getaway, the ranch was transformed into multiple accommodation options, including upscale log cabins. Visitors can take tours of the farm every morning or book dinner at the fine dining restaurant.

Tip: Brush Creek Ranch is about four hours from Denver International Airport. If driving from Denver, stop for lunch in Fort Collins, a charming university town often voted one of the best places to live in the United States.

QUOTABLE

"Brush Creek Ranch is the ultimate American ranch experience, without sacrificing any creature comforts. In fact, its culinary program is among the best in the country and there is a plethora of activities to engage any age and interest, all in a spectacular setting." —Jack Ezon, founder of Embark Beyond

OPPOSITE: Stretch and relax alongside playful—and lovable—baby goats during a yoga class at Brush Creek Ranch.

WASHINGTON, D.C., U.S.A.

THE HAY-ADAMS

A host to politicians past and present, this D.C. institution offers a luxe stay in the heart of the nation's capital.

YEAR ESTABLISHED: **1928** NUMBER OF ROOMS: **145** FAMOUS FEATURE: **Political history**
WHEN TO GO: **Year-round**

The importance of The Hay-Adams to American politics can be summed up in the name of its subterranean, dimly lit bar: Off the Record. Stories are always brewing in D.C.—whether or not they make it into the news cycle—and sometimes they stem from power drinks at this hotel's storied bar.

This is as close as you can get to staying at the White House. Built on the site of two historic houses—one belonging to John Hay, President Lincoln's private secretary, and the other to Henry Adams—it has hosted a slew of presidents, politicians, and visiting dignitaries. Barack Obama stayed with his family for nearly two weeks before moving in across the street.

A total of four rooms (including the Presidential and Federal Suites) on the seventh and eighth floors have White House views. And when the leaves fall in winter, the sixth floor (and two more rooms) get a view of the famous home, too.

But even if you're not in one of these rooms, the hotel's rooftop has the city's most spectacular panorama. "Top of The Hay hosts the most beautiful special events, including decadent holiday brunches and the July Fourth dinner and fireworks," says Tiffany Dowd, founder of Luxe Social Media. "The ongoing Author Series luncheons and Music Salon series are always a favorite with local residents and guests."

Because the hotel welcomes a rotating circle of political powerhouses, Dowd says: "You never know who you might bump into at The Hay-Adams."

OPPOSITE: You'll see the president's home and the Washington Monument out your window during a stay in a White House View room at The Hay-Adams.

ASPEN, COLORADO, U.S.A.

HOTEL JEROME

At the center of Aspen's social scene for more than 100 years, this silver mining–era hotel has made its mark on the ski town.

YEAR ESTABLISHED: **1889** NUMBER OF ROOMS: **93** FAMOUS FEATURE: **The J-Bar**
WHEN TO GO: **Year-round**

For a so-called small town, Aspen has a lot going on—and the Hotel Jerome, a landmark of this Colorado ski town since 1889, remains the center of so much of the social life. Unlike many ski resorts in the world, Aspen is a year-round destination, offering the global appeal of a much bigger city with big-name galleries, including the 33,000-square-foot (3,066 m^2) Aspen Art Museum, which offers free entry.

At the base of Aspen Mountain is a compact and walkable grid, with a buzzing shopping and restaurant scene. Throughout the year, lifelong learners attend the Aspen Institute, a well-respected forum for sessions on executive leadership and philanthropy, history and climate change, literature, and music, as well as the annual Aspen Ideas Festival. Winter centers around skiing on one of four mountains: Aspen, Aspen Highlands, Buttermilk, or Snowmass. Summer brings endless hiking and biking options, along with big events like the Aspen Music Festival and the FOOD & WINE Classic.

Jerome B. Wheeler, who was a co-owner of the flagship Macy's in New York City, opened the hotel in the middle of Aspen's silver mining boom, which injected a huge amount of cash into the town. After the crash of 1893, the hotel fell into disrepair and became a boardinghouse. Aspen remained rather quiet until it started to make money in a different way—as a ski destination for international jet-setters.

Today, the redbrick Victorian facade remains a time capsule of Aspen's

ALTERNATE STAY

The Little Nell is Aspen's only ski-in/ski-out hotel option. Right at the base of Aspen Mountain, its ski-up Ajax Tavern is the place to be for après-ski lunch or dinner (don't miss the french fries) on the patio.

OPPOSITE: Aspen's powdery ski slopes are just minutes from your room at Hotel Jerome.

HOTEL JEROME

ABOVE: The lobby at Hotel Jerome is known for its plush fabrics and timeless details.

OPPOSITE: Dating back to the Colorado silver boom, the historic Hotel Jerome is a premier place to stay in Aspen during the ski season or offseason.

silver mining peak. The interior is eclectic American West with a touch of Ralph Lauren. The Living Room, with dim lighting, silver chandeliers, and leather chesterfield sofas, is the place for cozy cocktails. It also has a small outdoor pool and hot tubs for après-ski.

The hotel's J-Bar ranks as one of the world's great hotel bars and is famous for its Colorado beef burger served on a brioche bun. Counterculture figure and author of *Fear and Loathing in Las Vegas* Hunter S. Thompson loved the J-Bar and made it his unofficial campaign headquarters in 1970 when running for sheriff on the promise of legalizing drugs. Spoiler: He lost, but not by many votes.

PARADISE VALLEY, ARIZONA, U.S.A.

THE HERMOSA INN

Enjoy sunny days and stunning sunsets on the patio at this Southwest gem near picturesque Camelback Mountain.

YEAR ESTABLISHED: 1936 **NUMBER OF ROOMS:** 43 **FAMOUS FEATURE:** LON's Restaurant
WHEN TO GO: Year-round

The beauty of Arizona casts a spell, and in the town of Paradise Valley, it feels especially magical. This small desert oasis is bordered by Scottsdale, Phoenix, and various mountain ranges with about 13,000 residents. Nearly 300 days of sunshine a year give Arizona locals long, beautiful evenings on patios. The patio at the Hermosa Inn's main restaurant, LON's, is especially transportive at sunset, with soft outdoor seating, glowing firepits, and twinkly lights, surrounded by lush and colorful desert gardens.

LON's is consistently rated as one of Arizona's best restaurants. Cocktails are made with herbs from the on-site garden and have names like the Stetson, Blooming Saguaro, and Cowboy's Dream. As far as the food is concerned, it's "globally inspired Arizona cuisine" and involves cooking techniques such as smoking, charring, and grilling for southwestern flair. The menu largely focuses on seafood and meat, but delicious vegetarian options include a butternut squash "steak" with charred artichokes and almonds. For breakfast, order the house specialty, monkey bread, to share at the table. You'll want seconds of the large bun with caramel, pecans, and cream cheese icing. The breakfast tacos and burritos are a great taste of local flavor, or opt for healthier options like organic oats and avocado toast.

In nearby Old Town Scottsdale, art is a big draw. The area boasts more

WHILE YOU'RE THERE

If you're fairly fit, Camelback Mountain is the valley's most iconic hike. Two trails lead to the summit: Echo Canyon, a more difficult, sometimes vertical climb, and Cholla Trail, a longer but easier walk up. Both are reachable with a five-minute drive from the hotel.

OPPOSITE: LON's Restaurant at the Hermosa Inn offers a beautiful brunch table, including eggs Benedict and the hotel's famous monkey bread.

PAGES 192–193: Sit by the fire in the Hermosa Inn's warm lobby, decorated with classic southwestern architectural elements.

than 50 galleries worth perusing—try to time your visit to a Thursday evening ArtWalk, a weekly event where the public can freely explore many of the galleries.

Art is also part of the history of Hermosa Inn. In the 1930s, long before the inn opened to guests, artist Lon Megargee created this hideaway as his own private escape and workplace. The turret you see on the property was his former studio and has views of Camelback Mountain. You can explore each piece in the gardens and on the walls through a self-guided art walk.

Casitas and suites are warm and inviting with Southwest-style rugs, fireplaces, wood floors, leather seating, and hand-painted tiles. The best rooms have private patios to enjoy the weather—though LON's remains the most magical alfresco setting of all.

Tip: The peak time to visit is in March, when the orange blossoms are blooming and the air is warm during the day but cool at night. Rates drop significantly in the high heat of summer in the desert.

AFTER CHECK-IN

Do like the locals do and resort-hop for a drink or dinner in the Valley of the Sun. Options include the Frank Lloyd Wright–inspired Arizona Biltmore, Sanctuary on Camelback, the Royal Palms Resort and Spa, Four Seasons Resort Scottsdale at Troon North, and the Fairmont Scottsdale Princess (where the outstanding Christmas at the Princess event is an annual tradition for many).

MORRISTOWN, ARIZONA, U.S.A.

CASTLE HOT SPRINGS

Meant for rest and relaxation, this lesser known hideaway in the Sonoran Desert is an all-inclusive treat.

YEAR ESTABLISHED: **Originally built 1896; reopened 2019** NUMBER OF ROOMS: **30**
FAMOUS FEATURE: **Natural hot springs** WHEN TO GO: **Year-round**

The final seven miles (11 km) to Castle Hot Springs, an hour's drive north of Phoenix and Scottsdale, is on a bumpy dirt road. Fitting, as the first guests arrived here by stagecoach. Luckily, you're in an air-conditioned car and easily able to behold the Sonoran Desert dream from the passenger seat: a lush green oasis with towering mountains, set on 1,100 acres (445 ha) with more than 500 palm trees.

In a state boasting extraordinary luxury resorts, Castle Hot Springs is considered Arizona's first, centered around three natural hot springs with healing minerals that Indigenous tribes have used for centuries.

The original resort opened in 1896 and quickly became known as a health and wellness destination. Titans of industry including the Wrigleys, Roosevelts, and Astors visited for weeks at a time. During World War II, the hotel served as a rehab center for injured soldiers; future U.S. president John F. Kennedy spent several months here. In 1976, a fire destroyed the main hotel building. Later, an entrepreneur and Arizona history buff bought and completely restored the hotel, which reopened in 2019.

Among the accommodation choices are Sky View Cabins, where each deck comes with a telescope for stargazing, and the Wrigley Cottage, one of the last original buildings, dating back to 1908. The rooms have no TVs; your stay here is all about reconnecting in the desert. Instead of channel surfing,

MEET UP

After you leave Castle Hot Springs for other Arizona destinations like Sedona or the Grand Canyon, try to reserve an evening at the memorable Blazin' M Ranch. It's a joyful Wild West experience with a barbecue dinner followed by an hour-long variety show featuring award-winning musicians.

OPPOSITE: Walk 200 feet (61 m) across the desert floor along the Castle Hot Springs Via Ferrata adventure course.

ABOVE: **Bathe in the relaxing waters of a stone tub inside the Spring Bungalows.**

OPPOSITE: **Enjoy evenings in the Sonoran Desert by exploring Castle Hot Springs' luxurious outdoor spaces.**

take to the private hiking and e-bike trails or soak in the famous hot springs.

Three pools cascade down from the source of the hot springs. The top pool averages temperatures of 105°F (41°C), the middle one is 95°F (35°C), and the bottom one hovers around 85°F (29°C). Soaking in mineral water, rich in lithium and magnesium, is a pristine, grounding experience.

The hotel's incredible three-acre (1 ha) farm touches every aspect of the resort, from the herbs in the spa oils to 80 percent of the produce served on the property. They even grow sugarcane to make their own ice cream.

You must be a staying guest to enjoy the pleasures of Castle Hot Springs. Rates include breakfast, lunch, and dinner, as well as many activities and staff gratuity.

SANTA FE, NEW MEXICO, U.S.A.

THE INN OF THE FIVE GRACES

Design influences from around the world come together in this inspirational escape from day-to-day life.

YEAR ESTABLISHED: **1996** NUMBER OF ROOMS: **25** FAMOUS FEATURE: **Luminaria Villa** WHEN TO GO: **Year-round**

The five graces are a reference to a Tibetan philosophy that we are "graced with five senses to experience the splendor of the world," says Santa Fe's Inn of the Five Graces. And at the hotel, every sense is on fire. Set on a quiet street and built in formerly abandoned adobe buildings, the inn was brilliantly imagined and designed by Ira and Sylvia Seret, who also run the nearby Seret & Sons furniture store (pop over and pick out some new furnishings, like an antique leather chest, for your own home). The hotel is a perfect reflection of the cultural confluence that is Santa Fe: a mix of Native American, Spanish, and western and eastern influences.

The inn's rooms allow you to escape from normal life—they are a dazzling celebration of beauty and peace through global design with Afghan, Tibetan, and Southwest elements.

In the bathrooms, for instance, almost every inch is covered by hand-laid, colorful tiles, many pulled from the Seret family's private collection. The most luxurious accommodation option is the 2,000-square-foot (186 m^2) Luminaria Villa, which features five woodburning fireplaces and some of the building's original adobe walls and woodwork in the kitchen.

During your stay, don't miss the Pink Adobe, a stone's throw from the hotel and a Santa Fe tradition since 1944, for margaritas and enchiladas. The French onion soup and apple pie are also worth ordering.

OPPOSITE: Exquisite tile decorates the Luxury One-Bedroom Suite at the Inn of the Five Graces.

WALLAND, TENNESSEE, U.S.A.

BLACKBERRY FARM & MOUNTAIN

Acres and acres of working farmland provide the produce and history that have put this Great Smoky Mountains destination on the map.

YEAR ESTABLISHED: **1976** NUMBER OF ROOMS: **68** FAMOUS FEATURE: **Farm-to-table excellence**
WHEN TO GO: **April–June or September–November**

Down a country road in Tennessee, bordering Great Smoky Mountains National Park, lie two idyllic properties, Blackberry Farm and Blackberry Mountain. They sit on thousands of acres of well-protected pastoral paradise with rolling hills where sheep graze, pigs lounge under trees, and chickens run out on the golf cart paths.

Sandy and Kreis Beall purchased Blackberry Farm in 1976, and it operated as a small country inn for many years. Their son Sam Beall (who passed away in 2016) and his wife, Mary Celeste, led its evolution into one of the leading food- and wine-focused hotels in the world. In 2019, the team opened nearby Blackberry Mountain, which focuses more on adventure and wellness.

The extraordinary gardens program focuses on preservation, as well as honoring the traditions of farming in East Tennessee. Explore the history of naturally protected coves and valleys and the genetics of various seeds that have stayed within families and geographic areas.

For guests, the agricultural history keeps the menus interesting: An heirloom eggplant might pop up for a couple of weeks; a unique tomato for a few days. Beyond the farming, the estate also boasts one of the largest wine collections in the country, with more than 166,000 bottles in its cellar.

There are miles of trails. One popular two-mile (3.2 km) hike takes you to

AFTER CHECK-IN

At the top of Blackberry Mountain, a historic fire tower used for wildfire spotting has been transformed into the Firetower restaurant. It's the best place to have a cocktail at sunset. Two bookable Watchman Cabins nearby offer wilderness-focused stays with no television.

OPPOSITE: On the Family Exploration Hike, kids can learn about the flora and fauna of the Great Smoky Mountains.

ABOVE: The troll Leo the Enlightened sits with a spectacular view of the Great Smoky Mountains. The statue was built from local scrap wood.

OPPOSITE: Spend a serene evening outside the Carriage House during your stay in one of its four premium suites.

the 20-foot-tall (6 m) troll Leo the Enlightened, created by Danish artist Thomas Dambo.

Blackberry Farm has an annual calendar of events that includes cycling weekends, cooking schools (chefs like Thomas Keller and Daniel Boulud have hosted), and personal discovery weekends. The farm's excellent spa is the Wellhouse.

At Blackberry Mountain, it's all about crafting your own stay. The Hub activities center offers an art studio. Or opt for yoga, sound bathing, indoor rock climbing, and more. Nest, the first Joanna Czech–certified spa in the United States, offers the celebrity facialist's favorite treatments.

Across the two properties is a mix of historic and estate rooms, cottages, and private homes. All food is included in your stay, as are all wellness classes.

BLUFFTON, SOUTH CAROLINA, U.S.A.

MONTAGE PALMETTO BLUFF

A Lowcountry gem, this hotel offers family-friendly excursions and a lesson in the nation's history.

YEAR ESTABLISHED: **2016** NUMBER OF ROOMS: **170** FAMOUS FEATURE: **Biking trails**
WHEN TO GO: **March–June or September–November**

Set among 20,000 acres (8,094 ha) of South Carolina Lowcountry, the Montage Palmetto Bluff is a secluded oasis surrounded by protected freshwater lagoons that lead into the Atlantic Ocean. The word "Lowcountry" evokes a feeling that the hotel lives up to: hot and humid air in the summer, a distinct landscape of live oaks and magnolia trees, saltwater marshes, and wetland grasses.

Located near the golf resorts of Hilton Head, Palmetto Bluff is much closer to Savannah, Georgia—just 40 minutes—than to Charleston. The Palmetto Bluff Conservancy protects the land and ensures that it looks almost the same as it did centuries ago. The long history—first as fertile ground for Indigenous people and later the site of plantations and aristocratic mansions—is documented by hotel staff archaeologists who recognize that the region's success lies on the shoulders of enslaved people.

Today, the hotel is a perfect getaway for friends or families. It has camps for children, a working farm from which much of the food is sourced, a golf course, horseback riding, biking trails, multiple pools, and a fitness center.

All of the room options feel refined and elegant, with glossy dark wood furnishings contrasted by bright white exteriors. The dreamiest options are cottages with river or lagoon views and fireplaces—though those won't be needed if staying in the summer.

QUOTABLE

"Montage Palmetto Bluff is a true gem of the Lowcountry. With its vast network of bicycle paths that seemingly stretch into infinity, guests can explore the beautiful surroundings at their leisure. The unique cottages offer charming and authentic experiences, and at night, guests gather around the fire for s'mores." —Susan Zurbin-Hothersall, travel adviser

OPPOSITE: A cloud-speckled sky is reflected in the water outside the Lagoon View Cottages at Montage Palmetto Bluff.

KIAWAH ISLAND, SOUTH CAROLINA, U.S.A.

THE SANCTUARY AT KIAWAH ISLAND

Whether you're looking to relax or play, this private island retreat is a hole in one.

YEAR ESTABLISHED: **2004** NUMBER OF ROOMS: **255** FAMOUS FEATURE: **Five golf courses**
WHEN TO GO: **March–June or September–November**

A day on Kiawah Island, 20 miles (32 km) south of Charleston, is best bookended with a beach bike ride. With the island's more than 10 miles (16 km) of hard-packed beach, it is delightful to cycle at sunrise or sunset directly along the Atlantic Ocean.

This barrier island boasts maritime forests (where oaks, palmettos, and palm trees thrive), and marshes and ponds encircle the bike and walking paths. Kiawah Island, named for the Kiawah tribe, is brimming with vibrant and fascinating wildlife, from fiddler crabs to turtles, foxes, bobcats, and birds.

In 2004, The Sanctuary at Kiawah Island opened, offering much needed resort elements to the island: a plush spa, cool cocktails and dining options, grand staircases, and polo shirts at the gift shop. Of the 255 rooms and suites, most have ocean views and a private terrace.

The island is private. Though The Sanctuary has gated security, anyone can book to dine, enjoy the spa, or play golf. After all, this is one of the world's premier destinations for golfers, with five 18-hole courses that are often compared to those in Ireland or Scotland. The Sanctuary's Ocean Course is considered to be one of the world's best.

Golf or not, plan on sunset porch drinks at The Ocean Course, overlooking the first tee and a Rolex clock, now an icon of Kiawah. In summer, don't miss the Mingo Point Oyster Roast and BBQ on Monday evenings.

ALTERNATE STAY

Combine Kiawah with a stay in Charleston, where the hotel scene has accelerated in recent years. Among the boutique hotel options are the Dewberry, Zero George, the Pinch, and the Planter's Inn, known for the 12-layer coconut cake at its Peninsula Grill.

OPPOSITE: The sixth hole at The Ocean Course, one of five golf courses at The Sanctuary at Kiawah Island

NANTUCKET, MASSACHUSETTS, U.S.A.

WHITE ELEPHANT

On an island that already screams Americana, this 20th-century hotel amps up storybook charm.

YEAR ESTABLISHED: **1923** NUMBER OF ROOMS: **66** FAMOUS FEATURE: **Brant Point Grill**
WHEN TO GO: **March–June or September–November**

Herman Melville wrote in *Moby-Dick,* "Nantucket! See ... how it stands there, away offshore." Fitting, because in the language of the Wampanoag, the Indigenous people of this small island (just 14 miles [23 km] long by 3.5 miles [5.6 km] wide), Nantucket means "faraway land." And upon arrival, you'll feel a world away from the mainland.

For at least two centuries, Nantucket was the whaling capital of the world. Today, the look of Nantucket epitomizes a classic New England seaside retreat with shingled, white-trimmed buildings.

Even with the hordes of crowds that descend during peak summer season, the island's well-preserved storybook charm remains. In 1975, the Nantucket Historic District area was expanded to cover the entire island with cobblestoned streets, ice-cream parlors (waiting in line at the Juice Bar is a ritual), and gift shops. Away from town, the beautifully pristine landscape feels like a time capsule of the whaling days and a more desolate island.

More than a century ago, socialite Elizabeth T. Ludwig began buying up a collection of rickety old houses and buildings, wanting to turn them into a high-end hotel. The general consensus was that this was her "white elephant," a total waste of money and time. If only those naysayers could see it now. Current owners Stephen and Jill Karp have been going to Nantucket for many years. It was fitting that they took up Ludwig's charge.

White Elephant, a harborside composite of the buildings Ludwig bought, is now a Nantucket icon. Three different sections make up the place: the

OPPOSITE: The pristine touches and crisp white bedding make the Harborview Suite at White Elephant one of the finest rooms in Nantucket.

PAGES 210–211: Guests can sit in a ring of comfortable lounge chairs and look out onto the stunning harbor.

PRIDE

hotel, the cottages, and the inn. In 2023, timed with the hotel's 100th anniversary, they unveiled a complete refurbishment of 54 rooms and 11 cottages. Incorporated into the new decor are coastal blues and sea greens, playing off the island's light and seafaring traditions. The elephant symbol is everywhere, from doorknobs to chair fabric in the library to the pillowcases in the bedrooms. The cottages are all named after and inspired by local Nantucket flora—Hydrangea, Snapdragon, Bayberry, and more.

Dinner on the patio at Brant Point Grill feels as Americana as you can get: Children are running around in the grass; boards are set up for cornhole; a flag proudly waves over the harbor and its hundreds of boats; and you'll find a choice of outdoor teak loungers by Arhaus with custom cushions made in White Elephant's signature blue.

One beloved ritual on Nantucket, open to anyone by reservation, is lunch or dinner at Topper's, located at sister hotel the Wauwinet, which opened in 1988 and is a 20-minute drive from White Elephant. It's a perfect adults-only retreat.

AFTER CHECK-IN

White Elephant is perfectly situated to everything in town. But you can also use one of the complimentary hotel cars for short excursions, like to the enchanting cottages in 'Sconset. The Nantucket Whaling Museum offers a fascinating look at the island's history. Don't miss the casual food icons, including Something Natural and Provisions for picnic sandwiches and Handlebar Café for coffee.

UTAH, U.S.A.

AMANGIRI

This striking hotel allows guests to heal amid the dramatic landscapes of a southwestern desert.

YEAR ESTABLISHED: 2009 **NUMBER OF ROOMS:** 44 **FAMOUS FEATURE:** Health and wellness
WHEN TO VISIT: Year-round

A legion of hotel fans known as "Aman Junkies" try to stay at as many Aman properties as possible. They are drawn to Aman's ethos of high design meets sustainable modernity. (The collection's name is derived from a word meaning "peace.") Amangiri, in southern Utah, is no exception. The hotel has become world-famous for its striking architecture, a horizontal stretch of structures that seemingly disappears into the desert landscape. And guests love that it is essentially in the middle of nowhere. Amangiri is a four-hour drive from Las Vegas or a regional flight to Page, Arizona, then a 25-minute drive.

Immersing yourself in the landscape is the point. Try guided slot canyon tours and a number of via ferrata routes, a concept invented in the Italian Alps that utilizes rungs and cables to allow you to scale mountains.

The hotel offers two types of accommodations: the classic Amangiri pavilions and the newer Camp Sarika tents, a five-minute buggy ride away. (These aren't your day camp tents; this is luxury tenting.) Each section of the hotel has a pool, and some rooms have their own plunge pool. Dining is exceptional, with outlets offering Southwest-inspired cuisine (think Colorado River trout or northern bison spring rolls) and spectacular outdoor seating. At the spa, many treatments are connected to the landscape. Try the Grounding Ritual, which involves extensive breath work and meditation.

The room rate includes three meals a day for two people; also included are seasonal offerings like evening chats with Navajo elders. And while this is a honeymoon favorite, children of all ages are welcome.

OPPOSITE: The unique pool at Amangiri curves around a large sandstone rock jutting out from the surrounding desert.

MEXICO CITY, MEXICO

LAS ALCOBAS

Mexico City's chic boutique property provides a personal connection to the region.

YEAR ESTABLISHED: **2010** NUMBER OF ROOMS: **35** FAMOUS FEATURE: **Local flavor**
WHEN TO VISIT: **Year-round**

Born and raised in Mexico City, hotelier Samuel Leizorek has brought the passion for his hometown to Las Alcobas, a much adored luxury hotel that elevated the already charming, upscale neighborhood of Polanco when it opened.

The hotel's rooms and public spaces feature artwork and rugs by contemporary Mexican artists. And the accommodations are grand: Among the 35 rooms are three penthouse suites with open terraces. Turndown offers sweet locally made treats, artisan bath products are made with local ingredients, and the spa menu offers a signature Maya healing treatment.

One of Polanco's best restaurants is in the hotel. Anatol is leading the charge with high-end, seasonally driven Mexican dishes and in-house baked pastries for the guest-only breakfast.

Steps from green parks and some of the city's best restaurants and shopping, Las Alcobas is the ideal base to explore Mexico City by foot (key to avoiding Mexico City's notorious traffic). Take a stroll to indulge in the café culture, with lots of alfresco sidewalk seating. To showcase the best of Mexico City to guests, the hotel created Las Alcobas Experiences, offering half- and full-day tours highlighting the city's art (Diego Rivera, Frida Kahlo, and more), plus history, architecture, and cuisine. Don't miss Las Alcobas' taco tour.

OPPOSITE: Las Alcobas' presidential penthouse boasts a cozy fireplace and stunning views of downtown Mexico City.

RIVIERA MAYA, MEXICO

HOTEL ESENCIA

Not just a spot on the beach, this standout in Riviera Maya offers art, healing, and delicious food that will have you coming back for seconds.

YEAR ESTABLISHED: **2014** NUMBER OF ROOMS: **48** FAMOUS FEATURE: **Extraordinary villas**
WHEN TO GO: **Year-round**

For Kevin Wendle, the work of owning Hotel Esencia—a captivating, low-key beachside hideaway between Playa del Carmen and Tulum in Mexico's Riviera Maya—is deeply personal.

"You can find a bed and a beach anywhere," Wendle says. "I want to give people an experience, give them a menu of what is possible for the day. My staff and I think of each guest as if they are the most important person in our lives—parents, sisters, brothers—and think about how we want them to enjoy Hotel Esencia."

In a past life, Wendle worked as a Hollywood producer (*Fresh Prince of Bel-Air*, among other projects) and tech entrepreneur, but always loved real estate. After a few visits to Playa del Carmen, he bought Hotel Esencia, the former home of an Italian duchess. "I thought, This is the best beach in Playa del Carmen," he says.

The original villa, now the Main House, was "quite charming," but he wanted to elevate everything and brought in pieces of his personal art collection. "I wanted it to feel like it belongs to somebody, and now it really belongs to everybody who comes to enjoy it." From the Main House, an array of breezy beach, jungle, and pool villas, as well as suites, are studded across the property's tropical gardens and on the beach.

A top team of global creatives and designers has helped make this place what it is: CS Valentin brought in the iconic yellow beach chairs and spear-headed the website with signature illustrations by Pierre Le-Tan. Today,

OPPOSITE: At Hotel Esencia's Taiyo, enjoy Japanese dining with a Mexican twist.

PAGES 218–219: Stay in a luxurious beach suite for access to private beachfront terraces on the soft, white sand.

creative director (and former graphic designer for Chanel) Juan Carlos Gutierrez Chavira leads the way. Giancarlo Valle did the interiors of the newer 12,000-square-foot (1,115 m^2) villa, which has three swimming pools, an underground speakeasy, and a 20-person cinema.

Mapping out a day here is hugely satisfying. Simply sit on the beach and read a book, or get active by snorkeling or visiting caves. On the property, swimming with the manatees in the freshwater lagoon is a beloved tradition.

"Healing and wellness are a big part of what we do," says Wendle, "everything from organic elements to the latest in technology." The Maya-influenced spa grows herbs and flowers to use in the treatments, many inspired by ancient rituals.

Menus are centered around simple, perfectly prepared food such as grilled fish and vegetables. Esencia is known for fresh ceviche and juices, as well as a Japanese-style restaurant and an outpost of Riccardo Giraudi's Beefbar, originally from Monaco.

Many guests return to Esencia time and again; in fact, 52 percent are repeat guests, including some who have visited 10 or more times. It's not hard to see why.

AFTER CHECK-IN

"Off-property, there is a world of adventure," Kevin Wendle says. Explore the area's Maya history and ruins, including a tour of the ancient city of Chichén Itzá, one of the new seven wonders of the world. Or head to Tulum to see how this laid-back beach town has changed.

ST. BART'S, SAINT BARTHÉLEMY

EDEN ROCK

The first hotel on a once little known island, this indulgent beach treasure is now the place to see and be seen.

YEAR ESTABLISHED: **1950** NUMBER OF ROOMS: **41** FAMOUS FEATURE: **The Pippa Suite**
WHEN TO GO: **November–April**

Perched on a literal rock that juts out from a sandy beach and is surrounded by turquoise blue water, Eden Rock—part of the Oetker Collection—has one of the most dramatic locations of any hotel in the world.

It all started in 1945, when Rémy de Haenen became the first person to land a plane on St. Bart's, quite the achievement at the time. (Even today, landing here is not for the faint of heart: The airport has one of the shortest commercial runways in the world.) After his arrival, Haenen bought the piece of land that Eden Rock sits on today. Its purchase price: $200—no one wanted it. Joke's on them. Eden Rock became the first hotel on the island, long before St. Bart's became synonymous with international jet-setters. Notable people, including Greta Garbo and Howard Hughes, were among the first of Eden Rock's famous guests.

Today, Eden Rock is owned by Pippa Middleton's father-in-law, David Matthews. The Pippa Suite, in her honor, has decor inspired by a superyacht.

As Indagare founder Melissa Biggs Bradley, says: "I can think of few places in the world where the beautiful somehow become more lovely or the old feel younger—and in St. Bart's they all do." Everyone feels like the best version of themselves, surrounded by French joie de vivre and numerous wonderful restaurants. Guests might frolic at the beach bar's frosé trolley, delight in fresh doughnuts at breakfast, or indulge in lobster salad with champagne dressing for lunch. *À votre santé!*

OPPOSITE: A large freestanding tub and tiled room make the Villa Rockstar bathroom one of the finest in the Caribbean.

Eden Rock
Eden Rock
Eden Rock
Eden Rock

MAUNDAYS BAY, ANGUILLA

CAP JULUCA

With all the charms of a family-owned property, this hotel has modern luxuries and pristine beaches that take your stay to the next level.

YEAR ESTABLISHED: 1988 **NUMBER OF ROOMS:** 108 **FAMOUS FEATURE:** Pimms
WHEN TO GO: December–April

"Arriving on Anguilla makes you feel like a Bond villain because you usually arrive by boat via St. Maarten—it's an incredibly fun way to get into island mode," says Christina Riggio, who has returned to "warm and joyful" Anguilla multiple times for family holidays over the last two decades. The island has around 30 beaches, but Cap Juluca's beach is known as one of the best in the world, and "it is not overhyped," she says.

Since 2017, Cap Juluca has been owned by Belmond, but it all began with one couple, Linda and Charles Hickox, who owned the hotel for more than 30 years. While boating around Anguilla, they found a dream spot, Maundays Bay, where they decided to open a restaurant, Pimms—still a resort icon today. Then came villas and suites in the style of an all-white Greco-Moorish dream, designed by Los Angeles architect Oscar Farmer. Think domes, courtyards, and horseshoe arches with seamless indoor/outdoor living. After the Belmond acquisition, a new team of architects renovated and reimagined the property, adding new rooms and reinforcements to protect against storms.

Set on a crescent-shaped mile-long (1.6 km) stretch with the softest sand and warm aquamarine water, this is a place where your shoulders relax and where you can explore private coves, lounge on beach chairs, or dip into the bath-temperature water. It still has the soul of a family-owned property but now offers the luxuries that a global hotel brand can provide, including

OPPOSITE: Step from the turquoise ocean into a private pool at one of Cap Juluca's private pool villas.

PAGES 224–225: Horseback ride with friends along one of Anguilla's beaches.

a deeper commitment to sustainability through a corporate mission to protect natural resources and cultural heritage on the island.

Each room, including entry-level options, has ocean views and direct access to the beach. The top-tier suites and villas have private pools as well. Every night, guests find a new little treat, such as a homemade muffin or biscuit, on their pillows.

Aside from Pimms, you'll also find Cap Shack, a 10-minute walk from the hotel on the other side of the beach, where they serve some of the best fish tacos you'll ever have. As a nod to another beloved hotel in the Belmond portfolio—the Hotel Cipriani in Venice (page 18)—Cip's by Cipriani has food inspired by everywhere from the "Venetian canals to the shore of Maundays Bay."

One caveat? "Here, it is more about the beach than pool life," says Riggio. Though it has pool options, you may want to consider another property if you don't love beach time—but this crown jewel of a beach might quickly change your mind.

DRINK IT UP

"A fun local spot is Bankie Banx's Dune Preserve, a beach bar owned by reggae artist Bankie Banx," says Christina Riggio. "He runs it with his son, has local musicians play, and makes very strong tropical drinks." She also recommends Blanchard's, a family-owned beachfront bistro, for freshly caught local fish.

QUÉBEC CITY, QUÉBEC, CANADA

FAIRMONT LE CHÂTEAU FRONTENAC

A world-famous icon, this towering and grand hotel offers a taste of Québec City's culinary scene and French history.

YEAR ESTABLISHED: **1893** NUMBER OF ROOMS: **610** FAMOUS FEATURE: **Dufferin terrace** WHEN TO GO: **Year-round**

One of the most photographed hotels in the world, Québec City's grande dame defines the skyline as a turreted palace of more than 600 rooms perched on a historically important cliff overlooking the St. Lawrence River.

Samuel de Champlain, called the "father of new France," built a fort here in 1608 to defend his new settlement, Québec. But it was an important railway line, the Canadian Pacific (which later merged with Fairmont Hotels), that opened a grand hotel here. Inspired by the châteaus in France, Le Château Frontenac opened in the late 1800s for train travelers crisscrossing the Canadian Rockies. The hotel has played an important role in history since: In 1943, the hotel hosted the Quebec Conference, where leaders including Franklin D. Roosevelt and Winston Churchill strategized their military approach in WWII.

In the center of Old Québec City, a UNESCO World Heritage site with centuries-old architecture, you can walk the 2.9-mile (4.6 km) path around the old city walls, enjoying many historic vantage points. Running the length of the hotel's property is the Dufferin Terrace. It's a quintessential Québec City experience to promenade along the long wooden sidewalk.

OPPOSITE: Admire the recently renovated lobby along with historical artifacts displayed in specially designed cases.

PAGES 228–229: Evening light falls over Fairmont Le Château Frontenac and Québec City.

Whether or not you're staying the night, book the breakfast buffet at the Place Dufferin on the terrace. Other memorable restaurants, including a casual bar and high-end fine dining, are also open to anyone, guest or not.

The Québec culinary scene is defined both by its French roots (you'll find crepes and cassoulets) and the fertile landscape that surrounds the city. The nearby Île d'Orléans is bursting with small producers, including apple cider mills, wineries, cheesemongers, and lavender farms. And Québec's most beloved dish, poutine—french fries smothered in gravy and cheese curds—is on offer at Le Château Frontenac, served with pulled beef cheek and pickles to offset the richness.

Despite its size, the hotel now operates as a carbon-neutral property, specifically offsetting emissions by planting trees in nearby Montmorency Forest and working with a local historic university to ensure neutrality is achieved.

Think about booking a Fairmont Gold room, which includes private check-in, lounge access, and snacks throughout the day. Higher floor rooms mean better views.

AFTER CHECK-IN

Don't miss North America's oldest grocery store, J.A. Moisan, founded in 1871, with a timeless exterior and interior. Pack a shopping bag with local jams, fresh bread, and cheese from Île d'Orléans and set up a picnic in the popular Plains of Abraham park for views of Le Château Frontenac and the river.

FOGO ISLAND, NEWFOUNDLAND, CANADA

FOGO ISLAND INN

Community is everything at this one-of-a-kind hotel standing on the edge of the world.

YEAR ESTABLISHED: **2013** NUMBER OF ROOMS: **29** FAMOUS FEATURE: **Community enterprise**
WHEN TO GO: **Year-round**

Can small villages be saved from the relentless onslaught of globalization and preserve their sense of community, soul, and belonging? The remote, luxurious Fogo Island Inn proves that, yes, it is possible to revive a small community and help it thrive.

"There is inherent value in rural places that can be reclaimed and made relevant for 21st-century life, and losing our small communities and the human ways of knowing they contain is neither inevitable nor necessary," proclaims its website.

The operation stems from Zita Cobb's love of her hometown. An eighth-generation Fogo Islander turned tech entrepreneur, she founded the charity Shorefast (a term for the line used to attach a cod trap to the shore), which returns 100 percent of its profits to Fogo Island for reinvestment in the community.

With just more than 2,000 people living on the island, the population is largely supportive and extremely proud of Fogo Island Inn. Guests are paired with lifelong islanders through the Community Host Program to learn about the island's culture from a new friend. The half-day program is automatically built into every stay.

A total sense of place is at the core of every design element of the hotel, too. Architect Todd Saunders, a Newfoundlander, felt the "same burden as we feel to place," Cobb has said. The result is a distinctive contemporary building, with sustainable practices built in, that takes inspiration from historic island structures, most strikingly the wooden stilts. (The first European

OPPOSITE: Perched on stilts, Fogo Island Inn dramatically stands atop the North Atlantic coast.

PAGES 232–233: Visitors to the stark white Dining Room are awarded with fantastic views of the ocean.

settlers on Fogo Island were expected to return home, so homes were built to be temporary, hence the stilts.) Most of the furniture was designed and created on the island; quilts were made by local artisans. Many products in the hotel can also be purchased, further supporting the community. A 37-seat cinema shows documentaries about local culture (along with box office hits), and a cozy library is filled with books about Newfoundland and Canada.

Aside from the social enterprise and singular architecture, why come to this wild corner of the world? For astounding North Atlantic views, of course. Here you'll have sightings of icebergs, whales, and the northern lights—as well as "seven seasons" to explore, including pack ice in March, when pieces break off from Greenland and float down to the island; trap berth in June, reflecting the cod trap fishing history of the island; and berry in September and October for juicy blueberries, raspberries, and more. Food at the inn is hyperlocal, with a goal to source 80 percent directly from the island.

BEFORE CHECK-IN

You're not just going to stumble upon the Fogo Island Inn; the journey is part of the stay. It all begins in Gander, Newfoundland. From Gander, you can drive an hour to the Farewell Ferry for an hour's crossing, then another 30-minute drive to the hotel. Or you can charter a helicopter directly from Gander to the inn.

NORTH AMERICA & THE CARIBBEAN

BONUS STAYS

ANTIGUA

Jumby Bay Island, *Jumby Bay Island*

This all-inclusive car-free private island is colloquially known as the "Queen of the Caribbean" and is a seven-minute ferry ride from Antigua. Managed by Oetker Collection, the island is the ultimate indulgence, with a range of villas and suites plus activities like snorkeling, tennis, and a superb kids' club. The Jumby Bay Hawksbill Project has monitored the endangered hawksbill turtle colony since 1987, working to protect and increase the population.

CANADA

Wickaninnish Inn, *Tofino, British Columbia*

An unparalleled wild and luxurious retreat, the Wickaninnish Inn paved the way for tourism to Tofino Bay on Vancouver Island's Pacific coast. It opened in 1996, and every room has panoramic ocean views and cozy fireplaces. The appeal is in the connection to the surrounding nature and explorations into the unspoiled Canadian wilderness—hiking, whale-watching, birding, water sports, and more. The food and wine offerings are an integral part of the Relais & Châteaux experience.

MEXICO

Hacienda de San Antonio, *Colima*

One of Mexico's most beautiful estates, this pink hacienda—formerly the site of a 19th-century coffee plantation—has shaded corridors, distinct arches, and gardens inspired by the Alhambra palace in Spain. Set in the lush green foothills of the Colima volcano, each of the 25 rooms features colorful, handcrafted Mexican textiles, pottery, and paintings. Guests can tour the hacienda's 5,000-acre (2,023 ha) working ranch, Rancho Jabali, to see cheesemaking, coffee roasting, and wild horses roaming.

TURKS AND CAICOS

Beach Enclave, *Providenciales*

Part luxury hotel, part full-service villa, the family-owned Beach Enclave offers three locations in Turks and Caicos—Long Bay, Grace Bay, and North Shore. Each offers stunning houses with a range of bedrooms as well as amenities like a gym and a bar. Owner Vasco Borges has lived on the island for more than two decades and is passionate about travelers seeing the local side of Turks and Caicos—and having access to the best beaches and water activities.

COMO Parrot Cay, *Parrot Cay*

A 30-minute private ferry whisks you to Parrot Cay, a 1,000-acre (405 ha) island property founded by hotel magnate Christina Ong as one of her first COMO hotels in 1998. It is an iconic Caribbean

OPPOSITE: A candlelit dinner is served at the cozy Yellow Bar at Hacienda de San Antonio in Colima, Mexico.

PAGES 236–237: Relax on Parrot Cay, a private luxury island with beach houses and private residences in Turks and Caicos.

retreat with a whitewashed main building overlooking the beach club and soft ivory sand. The azure water looks equally filtered and unreal, a hallmark of Turks and Caicos. The Shambhala Spa is one of the most transformative wellness destinations in the Caribbean.

UNITED STATES

1 Brooklyn Bridge, *New York, New York*
New York has exploded in the last two decades, and 1 Brooklyn Bridge proves the city is a five-borough destination that doesn't only revolve around Manhattan. The hotel's vibe is green industrial chic (1 Hotels is a brand built on high sustainable standards); rooms with unforgettable bridge views are worth the investment. The rooftop pool and bar offer dazzling views of Manhattan's skyline, but Brooklyn has more than enough to keep you on this side of the bridge.

The Driskill, *Austin, Texas*
Long before Austin's real estate prices skyrocketed, the Driskill was a bastion of Texas hospitality, welcoming guests since 1886. Today, its location on Sixth Street means you are close to the taco joints, quirky shops, and music venues that have made Austin a beloved travel destination and the "Live Music Capital of the World." On the other side of the river, the concrete cool South Congress Hotel is another great option.

Grand Hotel Mackinac Island,
Mackinac Island, Michigan
Car-free Mackinac Island is accessible

HOTEL
EMMA

ABOVE: Diners engage in lively conversations at Contessa, a modern restaurant atop the Newbury in Boston.

OPPOSITE: The historic Hotel Emma, bathed in evening light, is located in San Antonio's Pearl District.

PAGES 240-241: When you stay at the Wickaninnish Inn in Tofino, Canada, find great surfing at Chesterman Beach.

only by ferry or small plane. Once you get here, walk, bike, or take a horse-drawn carriage. The nearly 400-room Grand Hotel Mackinac Island is the undisputed icon of the island and has been operating since 1887. With the longest hotel porch in the world, it invites guests to kick back, relax, and enjoy a Michigan summer—plus some of the island's famous fudge. Keep in mind the hotel closes during winter months.

Hotel Emma, *San Antonio, Texas*
The Pearl complex, a reimagined shopping and dining destination in what used to be the Pearl Brewery, has revitalized San Antonio, as has Hotel Emma, named for Emma Koehler, who ran the brewery with her husband. Designed by powerhouse Roman and Williams, the cavernous spaces and beautiful restaurants feel cozy and of the moment.

The Newbury, *Boston, Massachusetts*
First opened in 1927, the art deco property has evolved through several hotel brands before reopening as the Newbury. The hotel is vibrant and fresh

and is in arguably the best location in Boston, across from the townhomes of Beacon Hill and the leafy Public Garden—where the "Make Way for Ducklings" sculpture is forever a childhood favorite. The food is excellent, too. Book at the panoramic rooftop restaurant overlooking the city.

The Setai, *Miami, Florida*
Located right on Collins Avenue in the buzzy center of South Beach, Miami, the Setai is a serene mix of Asian style and service in a historic art deco building. The hotel is centered around a trio of temperature-controlled swimming pools and has one of the best alfresco courtyards to dine and drink in the city.

Sonnenalp, *Vail, Colorado*
A labyrinth of cozy corners and German charm, the Sonnenalp in Vail has been family-owned since 1979. With elements from the original property in Germany's Bavarian Alps, the hotel also offers excellent dining options, including a high-end restaurant open only in the winter and a Swiss option for fondue.

Sunset Key Cottages, *Key West, Florida*
A five-minute ferry ride from Key West, Sunset Key Cottages feels a world apart on its own private island. The hotel is made up of pastel-colored cottages. Catch the stunning sunset views at its long-running restaurant, Latitudes. Sleep in and enjoy the breakfast baskets delivered to guest rooms in the morning.

PART THREE

SOUTH & CENTRAL AMERICA

Stay at Awasi Patagonia (page 254) and experience the natural wonders of Torres del Paine on horseback.

TRANCOSO, BAHIA, BRAZIL

UXUA CASA HOTEL & SPA

With fishing huts turned luxury casas, you'll find a home away from home at this coastal destination.

YEAR ESTABLISHED: **2009** NUMBER OF ROOMS: **16** FAMOUS FEATURE: **Fishing huts**
WHEN TO GO: **December–May or October**

The arrival of UXUA Casa Hotel & Spa to Trancoso, once a sleepy fishing village on Brazil's Bahian coast, brought a chic spotlight to this tranquil corner of the world. But the area has not lost its soul; instead, the hotel has brought in more people who appreciate the local culture and can support the hotel's sustainability initiatives. The hotel was founded by Wilbert Das, the former fashion director at Diesel, and Bob Shevlin—both of whom are passionate about making a positive impact through education, environmental protection, local craftsmanship, and social mobility.

UXUA fits magically into Trancoso's quaint coastal scene with bright and colorful fishing huts, each unique, artisan-crafted, and inspired by the Native Pataxó culture. And the entire property is surrounded by pristine nature, rainforest, and vast white sandy beaches. "I love the idyllic beauty and true sense of place," says Maita Barrenechea, founder of MAI 10, a luxury South American travel agency.

Guests also love the casual yet chic atmosphere of UXUA, the design details, and the wellness aspect, with its nutritional spa and treatments based on ancient Bahian healing practices.

A stay at UXUA feels like the best version of a simple yet very fulfilling life: long beach days and evenings on the Quadrado as the sun sets, discovering new artists, and building community.

OPPOSITE: Restore your body with a trip to Vida Spa & Lab at UXUA.

JOSÉ IGNACIO, URUGUAY

VIK RETREATS

With options for architecture and art, horses and countryside, or beach and rest, this collection of properties has something for everyone.

YEAR ESTABLISHED: **2009** NUMBER OF ROOMS: **Varies by location** FAMOUS FEATURE: **Artisanal decor**
WHEN TO GO: **Year-round**

José Ignacio—often called the Hamptons of South America—is a beach town on Uruguay's Atlantic coast that attracts an upscale bohemian crowd seeking wild beaches, contemporary art and architecture, and delicious seafood caught fresh that day. The transformation from sleepy fishing village to coastal destination is in part due to Vik Retreats opening three dream properties in and around José Ignacio. Started by husband-and-wife team Alex and Carrie Vik, Vik Retreats now has six properties around the world, including two in Chile and one in Milan. But start your stay in Uruguay, where travelers often book a stay at all three.

For architecture lovers who want to be close to town, **Playa Vik** is the best option. "This is the perfect base to enjoy the vibe of the village and beaches of José Ignacio," says Maita Barrenechea, founder of MAI 10, a luxury South American travel agency. "It has a prime seaside location, facing the calmness of the blue ocean with memorable fiery sunsets on the horizon. The pool is a highlight, suspended and jutting into the ocean. The black granite bottom is gleaming in the night with optical lights mirroring the map of the stars of the Southern Hemisphere. The beautiful wooden bathtubs crafted from local canoes are the most inviting I've ever encountered."

Accommodation options include suites or casas with multiple bedrooms. All have striking and different contemporary art elements. Though all of the action of José Ignacio is within walking distance, the best spot for an evening

MEET UP

Within the luxury travel industry in South America, there is no greater expert than Maita Barrenechea, creator of personalized trips for decades. She is in the know, stylish, and honest—and has an unmatched book of contacts across the continent.

OPPOSITE: The impressive barbecue and artful dining area at Estancia Vik

PAGES 248–249: Lounge at Playa Vik's cozy firepit and watch the sun dip below the South Atlantic Ocean.

cocktail is at the hotel's sunken firepit, which offers plush outdoor seating and pillows.

Guests often combine a stay at Playa Vik with one at **Estancia Vik,** a great option for those who love art and a more countryside locale. This was the first of the three Vik properties in Uruguay and was originally a personal home for the Vik family. Today, it is still a working estancia, or ranch, in the heart of the Uruguayan countryside. But this 12-suite hotel also packs on the sophistication, with a focus on art. In fact, each room is designed by a different local artist.

Its destination is also key, as Barrenechea notes: "It offers the chance to live in the countryside, while being close enough to the beach and to the hinterlands where vineyards and olive plantations thrive. There are sweeping vistas of bucolic meadows—the perfect canvas to enjoy long walks across rolling plains. There is also a polo field to watch or learn about this fascinating sport. End the day with a barbecue in the boldly designed corrugated-iron barn sprinkled with colorful graffiti."

Aside from polo, outdoor activities abound, including bird-watching and horseback riding with gauchos across open grasslands.

CLOSE BY

A great add-on to a trip to Uruguay is a stop in Buenos Aires, Argentina. It is less than an hour's flight from Buenos Aires to Punta del Este, or you can take a ferry from Buenos Aires to Montevideo, which is a little more than two hours away. Spend a night in charming Montevideo before driving to José Ignacio.

ABOVE: **Visitors can enjoy a mural by Uruguayan artist Carlos Musso at Bahia Vik and the painted faces of the Vik family at this artsy hotel.**

OPPOSITE: **A horse grazes in front of the traditional Spanish-style facade of Estancia Vik.**

If your heart is set on the beach, then the largest of the three properties, **Bahia Vik,** is meant for you. The hotel is in the outskirts of the village, about a 20-minute walk from Playa Vik. As at its sister properties, rooms showcase the works of contemporary Uruguayan artists, with sleek and modern bungalows that offer deep soaking bathtubs inside and four shared pools outside.

"I love the setting, tucked in the rolling sand dunes with blades of seagrass swaying by the stretch of calm coastline," says Barrenechea. "Guests love the quiet retreat feel, with waterfront bungalows on an endless sandy beach."

Choose to relax on the beach or take part in one of the on-site activities, including yoga on the beach or paddleboarding. Or walk in to town or to the lighthouse, built in 1877.

ATACAMA DESERT, CHILE

TIERRA ATACAMA

Though views of the cosmos may draw you here, the hotel's mix of adventure and relaxation will have you seeing stars.

YEAR ESTABLISHED: **2008** NUMBER OF ROOMS: **32** FAMOUS FEATURE: **Stargazing**
WHEN TO GO: **May–July**

Chile's otherworldly Atacama Desert is known as being one of the best places in the world to stargaze thanks to virtually no light pollution. In this arid landscape, you'll see constellations and galaxies like the Milky Way as never before. The night sky is such a draw for stays that the Tierra Atacama hotel posts a calendar for astronomical events that range from meteor showers to Jupiter and Saturn appearing close together in the sky.

Annual rainfall here amounts to nearly nothing. The Atacama is the driest desert in the world, which usually makes being outside easy. The Tierra properties are self-proclaimed "adventure spa hotels," inspired by the passion of their owner, former Olympic skier Miguel Purcell, whose father owns Chile's famous ski resort Ski Portillo. The duality of adventure and spa encourages you to experience the surrounding landscape through hiking, on horseback, or by vehicle, and then return to the spa, Uma (meaning "water"), for treatments that incorporate local products such as sheep's milk and honey. If that's not enough, an infinity pool also overlooks the Licancabur volcano. All the chic rooms, with local Chilean touches like handmade blankets, also have a view of the volcano.

Sustainability is key here. Nearly 600 solar panels were installed to meet daily energy needs, the hotel has its own well and water treatment plant on-site, and they hire local apprentices to help train and educate in hospitality careers.

AFTER CHECK-IN

An hour from Tierra Atacama is the Atacama Large Millimeter Array (ALMA), the largest astronomical project in the world, with 66 antennae helping to map extraordinary discoveries in our cosmos, such as exploding supernova stars. Check for available weekend public visits.

OPPOSITE: Guests look out into the striking Atacama Desert landscape.

TORRES DEL PAINE, CHILE

AWASI PATAGONIA

Whether you're helping track pumas or enjoying a night under the stars, this far-flung hotel offers pure excellence in the form of nature and experience.

YEAR ESTABLISHED: **2013** NUMBER OF ROOMS: **14** FAMOUS FEATURE: **The Awasi Foundation**
WHEN TO GO: **October–April**

Located at the southern end of South America and the Andes mountain range, the vast, fjord- and glacier-filled Patagonia region is shared by Argentina and Chile. Awasi Patagonia is on the Chilean side, within Torres del Paine National Park. This hotel is one of the more remote options in this book; it is a two-hour, windy drive from the closest airport of Puerto Natales.

When you do make it here, though, you are paired with your own personal tour guide upon check-in. They'll lead you through all the excursions, which are personalized to your wants, whether long days of hiking or more tranquil pursuits.

Many guests opt to participate in early morning puma tracking, which allows you to at least try to spot the elusive big cat. The Awasi Foundation—funded by guests staying here—created a wildlife corridor just outside the protected national park by leasing additional land and expanding the area of protection. The goal is to restore the natural habitats of pumas, foxes, condors, eagles, and other wildlife that live here. There are more than 20 Awasi guides at the hotel during open season, but seven remain on-site in the winter to continue tracking behavioral patterns and movements to further the work of the foundation.

As for your stay, 14 luxurious bungalows blend into the terrain and allow you to enjoy the immense natural beauty. You'll also especially enjoy delicious food and wine after a day of exploration in a far-flung paradise.

OPPOSITE: Soak in a private wood-fired hot tub during a stay in one of Awasi Patagonia's serene villas.

PAGES 256–257: Awasi's spacious villas appear small beneath the behemoth mountains of Torres del Paine.

Awasi

"I love the low-impact design of the lodging and how the native timber-clad cabins manage to stand out and yet blend in," says Maita Barrenechea, founder of travel agency MAI 10. "They are aesthetically captivating in every detail and offer expansive views of the imposing granite spires of the Paine towers and the salty Lake Sarmiento. Guests love the utmost sense of comfort that is achieved in sheer wilderness, and the personalized explorations."

End the day in an outdoor hot tub—every suite has its own—heated with burning wood, which enriches the experience with the evocative smell of a campfire under the stars. There are certain places on Earth where a human being's senses are on fire. In Patagonia, with these mythical views, it is impossible to not feel moved.

Awasi is generally closed May through September for the winter season. The room rate is high (minibar included though!), and it has a three-night minimum stay, but the high price tag makes sense when considering the work it takes to operate and fund the foundation.

AFTER CHECK-IN

Spend a meaningful day hiking and exploring with an Awasi guide in the Sierra Baguales, a mountain range with fields of fossils, condors soaring overhead, and herds of wild guanacos. It makes people stop and say, "This is Patagonia"—wild, open areas with no one around except a gaucho or two herding cattle through the valley.

MENDOZA, ARGENTINA

CAVAS WINE LODGE

Sample the wine Mendoza is famous for while basking in an idyllic winelands hideaway.

YEAR ESTABLISHED: **2005** NUMBER OF ROOMS: **18** FAMOUS FEATURE: **Private roof terraces**
WHEN TO GO: **October–April**

South America's leading luxury travel expert, Maita Barrenechea, owner of travel agency MAI 10, was the first guest at Cavas Wine Lodge before it opened to the public in 2005—and she's loved it ever since. Billed as one of the top options in the region—the heart of wine country in Argentina—the hotel is set just 40 minutes from the leafy city of Mendoza, making it easy to explore the area's abundant restaurants and wineries. The wider region, at the foot of the Andes Mountains, is known for exporting Malbec—a great pairing with a high-quality Argentine steak—but also Chardonnay and Merlot.

As far as the hotel goes, Cavas Wine Lodge is the brainchild of Martín Rigal and Cecilia Diaz Chuit, who dreamed up their Spanish colonial-style resort with adobe-style villas long before Mendoza had any luxury accommodations.

"The lodge is just lovely and breathes romance in every corner," says Barrenechea. "Guests love its tranquility and idyllic setting. You walk through the vineyards to your hidden casita, explore the surrounding winelands, and return to your private oasis to take a dip in the pool or lounge on your roof terrace and enjoy a soothing sundowner with your fireplace lit and the sight of the sun falling behind the majestic, ever white Andes Mountains."

OPPOSITE: Sip fine wines by the fire on a private balcony at Cavas Wine Lodge.

CUSCO, PERU

PALACIO NAZARENAS

A home base on a trip to see Machu Picchu, this culturally inspired hotel will make you want to extend your stay.

YEAR ESTABLISHED: 2012 **NUMBER OF ROOMS:** 55 **FAMOUS FEATURE:** All-suite accommodations
WHEN TO GO: April–May or October–November

A special feature of many top hotels in Cusco, a UNESCO World Heritage site high in the Peruvian Andes, is oxygen tanks. Why? Some visitors feel a bit woozy upon arrival and need time to adjust to the altitude. At Palacio Nazarenas, A Belmond Hotel, every room is oxygen-enriched to assist in the transition to living at 11,152 feet (3,399 m) above sea level.

Cusco is a joyful and energetic city, with pink terra-cotta roofs and beautiful squares built among centuries-old Inca ruins. Spain invaded in the 1530s and stayed for around 300 years, destroying much of the Indigenous Inca culture and instead erecting baroque churches and buildings. That mix of Inca and Spanish culture and style is evident throughout the city and in Palacio Nazarenas itself, a restored 17th-century convent. The hotel sits a stone's throw from the beautiful Plaza de Armas at the center of the city and a short walk from the buzzy artist's neighborhood of San Blas. You'll find plenty of reachable excursions from your home base: For the best people-watching, head to the Mercado Central de San Pedro, explore the ruins at Sacsayhuaman, or go for dinner at Pachapapa—it's up to you whether you try the house specialty, roasted guinea pig.

During the hotel's restoration process, representatives from Peru's National

CLOSE BY

Bird-watchers will love the Sacred Valley too, with nearly 2,000 species of birds to discover. And everyone enjoys the beautiful Sunday markets. The Rio Sagrado hotel, a sister property to Palacio Nazarenas, overlooks the Urubamba River and feels soulfully close to the ancient Inca cultures that inhabited the area.

OPPOSITE: The hills of Cusco surround the lavish courtyard and pool area of Palacio Nazarenas.

Institute of Culture were on-site to find and protect any Inca ruins. You can see some of these treasures displayed behind glass as you walk through the cloistered white courtyards. To honor the region, rooms have soft alpaca throws and carved chestnut furnishings commissioned from local artists. The hotel also has the city's only heated outdoor swimming pool and a spa with treatments inspired by local customs and products.

Of course, Cusco is the launching point for the *Hiram Bingham* train to Machu Picchu, where you'll actually go down to 8,000 feet (2,438 m) above sea level. As the Andean landscape whizzes by, guests sit in brass- and wood-paneled seats with white linen tablecloths, enjoy local dishes, and sip on pisco sours. On the way home, passengers dance to the beat of the Peruvian *cajón* (box drum) in a party atmosphere.

You can take a long round-trip ride in one day, or you can stay the night at the only hotel next to Machu Picchu—the Sanctuary Lodge.

ABOVE: Expand your palate with a pisco sour tasting session at Palacio Nazarenas.

OPPOSITE: Take a day trip to Machu Picchu to explore the iconic Inca ruins.

COSTA RICA

NAYARA RESORTS

Built in the Costa Rican jungle, these three nature-set resorts offer the chance to explore the land of pura vida.

YEAR ESTABLISHED: **2008** NUMBER OF ROOMS: **Varies by location** FAMOUS FEATURE: **Three resort options**
WHEN TO GO: **December–April**

In the middle of 4,500 acres (1,821 ha) of rainforest, this trio of Nayara eco-retreats in Costa Rica looks out to Arenal Volcano National Park and embodies the country's motto: *pura vida*. Here you'll find great adventure and wellness options, coffee tastings, hot springs, wildlife sightings, and more—all with a globe-leading sustainability mission.

The first of the resorts to be built was **Nayara Gardens,** a family-friendly property with casitas. Next came the luxury villas and hot spring–fed plunge pools at **Nayara Springs,** which is for adults only. **Nayara Tented Camp** opened in 2022, with highly designed one- to four-bedroom canvas tents, inspired by classic safari lodges and built after a successful major reforestation project on the mountain.

Traveling on footbridges and pathways, guests can make their way between the hotels for more than 10 dining options, which vary from Costa Rican casual (rice bowls with black beans, ceviche) to Asian fusion. There are also two spas (book the volcanic mud massage, a perennial favorite).

Wildlife is abundant, and the hotels offer evening frog watch walks and an on-site sloth sanctuary, among other ways to explore Nayara's successful rewilding efforts.

All three properties are completely carbon neutral, and there is no plastic anywhere. Owner and sustainable travel leader Leo Ghitis prefers to frame these sustainability efforts as regenerative travel, leaving the area better than what it was. Nayara also provides its staff with free transportation and early childhood education.

OPPOSITE: **Relax in the open-air spa at Nayara Springs, where treatments incorporate locally grown coffee, chocolate, and volcanic mud.**

SOUTH & CENTRAL AMERICA

BONUS STAYS

ARGENTINA

Casa de Uco, *Mendoza*

In Argentina's Mendoza wine region, this is a "family dream project come true," says Maita Barrenechea, owner of luxury travel agency MAI 10. Father (Alberto Tonconogy) and daughter (Julia) shared the hotel's overall design vision; son (Juan) is the wine connoisseur. Sprawling vineyards surround the property, with views to the snowcapped Andes. "Horses and bicycles are ready to ride along endless lines of vines or across the desert wilderness," says Barrenechea.

Palacio Duhau - Park Hyatt Buenos Aires, *Buenos Aires*

Originally built as a palatial mansion in 1934 for the aristocratic Duhau family, this hotel seamlessly melds the glamorous historical building with a newer sleek tower in the posh neighborhood of Recoleta. Terraced gardens link the two. Come for a drink on the alfresco terrace or in the Oak Bar. This is a hotel of glam, with deep wood paneling, crystal chandeliers, and marble throughout the property.

The Vines Resort & Spa, *Mendoza*

If you love food and wine, this extraordinary hotel offers the best in the world, from Chef Francis Mallmann's wood-fired Argentine cuisine to incredible wine-tasting experiences. Oh, and snow-covered mountain views. "The gym floating over the winelands with wrap-around views of the vineyards makes for the most appealing place to exercise I can recall," says Barrenechea. The architecturally stunning property is located near several boutique wineries, including the family-owned SuperUco; Gimenez Riili; Corazón del Sol; Solo Contigo; and The Vines winery, which you can explore by bicycle, horseback, or car.

BRAZIL

Copacabana Palace, *Rio de Janeiro*

Recently celebrating 100 years of jet-setting glamour, this icon on Rio de Janeiro's Copacabana Beach featured in *Flying Down to Rio* starring Fred Astaire and Ginger Rogers. The "half-Olympic-size" pool is the heart of the property, though there is nothing like waking up to a view of the wide and expansive beach, where surfers rush into the waves and runners make their way down the famous mosaic-tiled promenade.

Ibiti Project, *Minas Gerais*

Set on a private family-owned reserve in the Brazilian state of Minas Gerais, the luxury accommodations (including an eight-room lodge, a villa, and cottages) support a mission of wildlife and ecological

OPPOSITE: Palacio Duhau — Park Hyatt Buenos Aires, located in the Recoleta neighborhood, features magnificent gardens and a two-building complex.

PAGES 268–269: Casa de Uco in Mendoza, Argentina, is surrounded by vineyards and views of the towering Andes Mountains.

preservation, plus social and economic initiatives. There is an organic farm with products for sale as well as wellness and art programs. It is a "well-guarded secret of the global jet set who seek meaning, connection, and transformation in their travels," says travel specialist Clark Kotula.

COLOMBIA

Casa Legado, ***Bogotá***

Owner Helena Davila has poured her heart—and design aesthetic—into this charming, art-filled 13-room boutique in Bogotá's upscale Quinta Camacho neighborhood. Located in two mid-century modern houses, the hotel has a wellness studio and cozy offerings, such as a movie night in the garden or pizza and raclette nights.

Casa San Agustín, ***Cartagena***

This chic and upscale 30-room property is built within three 17th-century buildings in the historic center of Cartagena. Highlights include a romantic outdoor pool, a spa, and a private beach a short drive away.

COSTA RICA

Pacuare Lodge, ***Limón***

Arriving at this 20-suite luxury tree house lodge sets the scene for an eco-vacation unlike any other—the easiest way to enter or exit is by white-water raft. The lodge is family owned with substantial sustainability cred, and adventures await, from zip-lining and bird-watching to cultural connections and chocolate tours.

ABOVE: Beachgoers enjoy a sunny day on Copacabana Beach, right outside Brazil's Copacabana Palace.

OPPOSITE: At The Vines Resort & Spa, savor the wines of Mendoza and regional dishes showcasing Argentine beef.

ECUADOR

Mashpi Lodge, ***Mashpi***

Just a few hours from Quito, Mashpi Lodge is a luxurious 22-room eco-stay made primarily of glass, allowing for endless rainforest and cloud forest views. An Ecuadorian businessman originally bought the land, which had been deforested, hoping to protect it. Now, it is a fully alive, diverse landscape once again. Hotel guests—and the money they spend here—help to preserve this special place.

Pikaia Lodge, ***Santa Cruz***

Most travelers see the Galápagos—and the fearless wildlife that inhabits the islands' beautiful ecosystem—from a boat, but Pikaia Lodge on Santa Cruz Island is so special that it warrants a pre- or post-cruise stay. The 14-room lodge leads an ambitious sustainability program that helps to reforest the land, a former cattle ranch. There are also top adventure and food options.

PANAMA

Islas Secas, ***Isla Secas***

Set on a 14-island archipelago, Islas Secas is a collection of one- to four-bedroom casitas (with no TV, but Wi-Fi) that are 100 percent powered on solar energy and focused on privacy. The collection also has an eye for local dining with Panamanian spices. Talk to the Adventure Concierge to explore the surrounding rich biodiversity.

PART FOUR

ASIA & THE MIDDLE EAST

Taj Umaid Bhawan Palace (page 292) is the perfect location to host a lavish wedding or celebration.

SUMBA, INDONESIA

NIHI SUMBA

Built with community at the forefront, this luxury hotel puts its plethora of sand and fun second to the local islanders.

YEAR ESTABLISHED: 2001 **NUMBER OF ROOMS:** 27 **FAMOUS FEATURE:** The Sumba Foundation **WHEN TO GO:** April–October

NIHI Sumba, located on the island of Sumba (more than double the size of Bali), has become a social media phenomenon. It's easy to see why: Wild horses galloping along a perfect beach make for compelling content. The resort is not easy to get to—after an hour-long flight from Bali, and then another two-hour car ride—but that is central to its appeal.

Before NIHI Sumba, the property was a pared-down surf camp and retreat called Nihiwatu, started by an American surfer who loved the waves in this remote part of the island. In 2012, businessman Chris Burch partnered with longtime hotelier legend James McBride to acquire the property and NIHI Sumba was born. The underlying goal of hotel operations is simple, admirable, and huge—to help the people of Sumba. The Sumba Foundation is funded by guest stays and aims to solve a multitude of problems for island dwellers, including nutrition, education, clean water, malaria, and more. Today, the resort is the main economic driver of the island. NIHI staff have connected themselves to the community on Sumba and are so protective of it. You feel that energy everywhere you go on the island.

Of course, there would be no stays to fund these honorable projects without an incredible experience for guests. The hotel comprises thatched-roof all-ocean-view villas. "The rooms are spectacular; it's very Indonesian and polished in a natural way," says Julia Perowne, owner of

OPPOSITE: At NIHI Sumba, the private outdoor bed of the Marangga villa looks out onto the Indian Ocean.

PAGES 276–277: Horses gallop across the white sand in front of NIHI Sumba.

Perowne International, a luxury brand consultancy. And though it offers feet-in-the-sand luxury, it doesn't take itself too seriously. The horses are integral to the stay: They lead sunset and sunrise rides and day trips to other parts of the island, or will swim with you at low tide. Children learn how to feed and groom the Sumba ponies through the Kids Pony Club, where they can also join regular chocolate-making classes. Anything in the water is possible, including surfing, fishing, and snorkeling.

Despite being beloved by honeymooners and privacy seekers, this is a deeply social place. "It's eccentric, it's fun, it's social," says Perowne. "You know you're going to meet the most interesting people when you're there. They have themed nights—like white night—and the energy is just so cool. We had most of our lunches with people we had met at dinner the night before."

AFTER CHECK-IN

Spa Safari™ (yes, it's trademarked) Nihioka is one of the most popular experiences at NIHI Sumba. "I think the experience is absolutely breathtaking," says luxury brand consultant Julia Perowne. "You're driven in open trucks to a little archipelago with no internet and one beautiful villa on the edge of a cliff with steps down to the beach. It's so incredibly romantic."

JERUSALEM, ISRAEL

KING DAVID HOTEL

Culture, religious history, and famous guests combine in this historic hotel in the heart of Jerusalem.

YEAR ESTABLISHED: **1931** NUMBER OF ROOMS: **19** FAMOUS FEATURE: **Views of Jerusalem's Old City**
WHEN TO GO: **Year-round**

This is the best located hotel in Jerusalem, with powerful, evocative views of the Old City. The list of notables who have stayed here is long and includes hundreds of kings, queens, presidents, Oscar winners, and more. But that celebrity appeal pales in comparison to the humble reality of being in the center of three monotheistic religions: Judaism, Christianity, and Islam. The spiritual hub is a destination for contemplating the depth and complexity of history and culture.

The holiest sites in the world for each of these religions are within walking distance of the hotel, as is the popular Mahane Yehuda market. It is worth booking a room with a view of the Old City to wake up and open the window to the sights and sounds of Jerusalem. A view of the Western Wall, beyond the hotel's palm trees and pool, is soul-stirring.

Hotels in Israel are known for their impressive breakfast buffets, and this one doesn't disappoint. You'll find a seemingly endless variety of local cheeses, salads, cereal, fruit, eggs, smoked fish, bread, and more. On Shabbat, the Jewish day of rest that lasts from sunset on Friday to sunset on Saturday, most of the city shuts down. At the King David, the gym and pool remain open, though the room service menu is more limited. Try to join the popular Shabbat dinner on Friday.

MEET UP

In such a complex, captivating destination, a knowledgeable tour guide is priceless. Meir More is one of the best in the city, personalizing his tours to your background and wish list, while also gently pushing you to think outside of what you know, weaving in stories from all the major religions.

OPPOSITE: The King David Hotel's splendid lobby is designed to highlight ancient Jerusalem history.

SINGAPORE

RAFFLES SINGAPORE

Home of the Singapore Sling, this city institution offers the suite life to its well-catered-to guests.

YEAR ESTABLISHED: **1887** NUMBER OF ROOMS: **115** FAMOUS FEATURE: **The Long Bar** WHEN TO GO: **Year-round**

"To have been young and had a room at Raffles was life at its best," James A. Michener, Pulitzer Prize-winning writer of *Tales of the South Pacific* and a regular guest of the hotel, once said. You'll likely agree with his sentiment as you step into the grand lobby—now adorned with a massive crystal chandelier after a total refresh. It is apparent that the historic glamour at Singapore's grande dame has been preserved, and a stay here feels like one of life's best moments—at any age.

The brand's first and flagship property is named for Sir Stamford Raffles, the founder of Singapore. Today, other "personality suites" are named for its most famous guests, including Elizabeth Taylor, Ava Gardner, and Pablo Neruda. All the rooms are suites, ranging from studio and courtyard options to promenade and grand hotel styles. If the hotel looks familiar, that's because characters Rachel Chu and Nick Young stay in the Sarkies presidential suite, named for the Armenian founders, in the hit film *Crazy Rich Asians*.

This is a place of history—including on its menu. In 1915, the iconic Singapore Sling was developed at the hotel's Long Bar. The drink was an instant hit with women, who at the time were not allowed to drink alcohol in public but could pass off this pink-hued cocktail as juice. The Long Bar is open to anyone (reservations recommended). The Writers Bar pays homage to famous authors who have stayed at Raffles, while the Tiffin Room has been a classic spot for dinner since 1892, serving up North Indian cuisine.

OPPOSITE: Narajan Singh, the legendary doorman, stands in front of the glamorous Raffles Singapore.

RAFFLES HOTEL

TOKYO, JAPAN

HOSHINOYA TOKYO

Offering Japanese traditions in the glass-and-steel capital city, this hotel is the perfect blend of past and present.

YEAR ESTABLISHED: **2016** NUMBER OF ROOMS: **84** FAMOUS FEATURE: **Sword training**
WHEN TO GO: **March–April or September–November**

At HOSHINOYA Tokyo, you must take off your shoes, which are carefully stored in lockers lining the walls. It feels incredibly special to cross a threshold into a distinctly Japanese *ryokan* (a traditional inn) just a short walk from Tokyo Station and the Imperial Palace and gardens.

"A lot of the hotels in Tokyo don't feel particularly Japanese," says travel writer Chadner Navarro. "But the spirit and energy of Japan is so apparent [at HOSHINOYA]. Every part of the experience is intentional, plus they add on so many things to your stay, like a tea lounge with different snacks and chocolates. I fell completely in love with it."

In other words, this is a place where the ryokan meets skyscraper, encapsulating both the history and innovation of Tokyo. The hotel is also distinctly Japanese, owned and operated by Hoshino Resorts, a fourth-generation family-owned brand.

Highlights include the 17th-floor rooftop *onsen* bath experience, where the water comes from underground hot springs. At 6:45 each morning, guests have the option to "refresh the mind and body" through sky-high morning *kenjutsu* practice (with skyline views). The time-honored tradition is a way to practice breath work. A delicious Japanese breakfast is served in a wooden box with grilled fish, salads, miso soup, and more.

You must be a staying guest to partake in this unique hotel's experiences, but it's well worth the cost of a reservation.

OPPOSITE: **A delicious, fresh breakfast is served at HOSHINOYA Tokyo.**

KYOTO, JAPAN

HIIRAGIYA KYOTO

Japanese hospitality, traditions, and cuisine are front and center at this centuries-old inn.

YEAR ESTABLISHED: **1818** NUMBER OF ROOMS: **28** FAMOUS FEATURE: **100-year-old rooms**
WHEN TO GO: **March–April**

Kyoto may be best known for sakura (cherry blossom) season in March and April, when the city draws tens of millions of visitors to see the famous blooms. But overall, the city feels more culturally traditional than avant-garde Tokyo (just over two hours away by bullet train). Kyoto also offers many more time-honored options for stays.

On any trip to Japan, you should spend at least one night in a *ryokan,* or traditional Japanese inn, where centuries-old hospitality standards are revered. The sixth-generation Hiiragiya Kyoto, established in 1818, is the ryokan you dream of. It has welcomed Elizabeth Taylor and Charlie Chaplin—and you can be its next star.

At Hiiragiya, service is exceptional to ensure guests feel like they're coming home—that is, a Japanese home, with its own customs including switching from shoes to slippers to preserve the traditional straw tatami mats. Rooms (some are more than 100 years old) are divided between the main building and the contemporary building. All are made with natural materials like wood, clay, paper, and ceramics. A cushioned futon replaces a table for bedtime. At breakfast, enjoy Japanese delicacies, including simmered tofu with fish, rice, and homemade pickles. Some Western options are also on the menu, if you wish.

Combine your stay with a more modern option, such as the ryokan-inspired Ritz-Carlton Kyoto or Hotel the Mitsui Kyoto.

ALTERNATE STAY

Paddy McKillen, the owner of contemporary art mecca Villa La Coste in Provence, France (page 108), recently opened the nine-room Shinmonzen in Kyoto. The hotel reflects his passion for art, with pieces by Louise Bourgeois and Damien Hirst, but it feels Japanese in style and service.

OPPOSITE: An intimate room in a *ryokan* serves many purposes, including being a bedroom, sitting room, and dining room.

BANGKOK, THAILAND

MANDARIN ORIENTAL, BANGKOK

The reigning grande dame of Bangkok, this is a see-and-be-seen hotel worth writing home about.

YEAR ESTABLISHED: **1876** NUMBER OF ROOMS: **331** FAMOUS FEATURE: **Bamboo Bar**
WHEN TO GO: **November–March**

The Mandarin Oriental, Bangkok—also known as "the Oriental"—occupies a stunning position on the edge of the Chao Phraya River, the same perch from which it has welcomed generations of royal families, world leaders, and society's elites since 1876.

The view of the mighty river is central to the experience here. Majestic and timeless, and infused with traditional Thai hospitality, the Oriental projects a sense of pride, elegance, and charm.

The 331-room hotel is divided into the River Wing, where most of the rooms have Chao Phraya views; the Garden Wing, added in 1958; and the Authors' Wing, which was the original hotel and now houses Authors' Suites.

The hotel has a strong literary connection. Some of its most famous guests include Joseph Conrad *(Heart of Darkness)*; W. Somerset Maugham *(Liza of Lambeth)*; and Noel Coward *(Blithe Spirit)*. Today, you can enjoy afternoon tea in the Authors' Lounge, flipping through books by famous literary guests with a finger sandwich and a cup of cold-brewed tea. (This is steamy Bangkok, after all.)

All rooms are outfitted with Thai silk from Jim Thompson Fabrics (the company's namesake helped popularize Thai silk in the 1950s and '60s), plus wood paneling and artwork.

Guests board teakwood shuttles to visit the Spa at Mandarin Oriental

OPPOSITE: At the Sala Rim Naam pavilion, just across from the hotel, dine on fine Thai cuisine and watch live performances.

PAGES 288–289: The two-bedroom Oriental Penthouse Suite offers expansive views of the Chao Phraya River and the city of Bangkok.

across the river. After, they can dine at one of the hotel's Thai restaurants close to the spa. Don't skip on an evening at the Bamboo Bar, open since 1953 and offering live music and jazz six nights a week.

Among the hotel's other highlights: two pools (one for children) that lend a resort-like feel to the property, a shopping arcade, and a vast breakfast buffet on the veranda overlooking the river.

"Evenings in the lobby are very special," says former general manager Amanda Hyndman, "and might be my favorite time at the hotel. You get wafts of heat and tropical smells and noises as the front doors continuously open and close. The lighting is low, the string quartet is playing, and it seems the whole world converges on the lobby to see and be seen."

After a day experiencing the city's chaos and beauty, returning to this lush oasis on the river and entering the double-height and wood-paneled lobby is completely restorative.

AFTER CHECK-IN

It may seem counterintuitive to say "go to the mall" for local culture in Bangkok, but that's exactly what you should do. Most visitors seek out Chatuchak, the weekend market with more than 1,500 stalls, but a visit to a mall is a surprisingly insightful look into modern Thai culture—plus malls have air-conditioning for a break from the city's heat. Visit Siam Paragon, an upscale shopping center with an aquarium, movie theater, restaurants, and more.

AGRA, INDIA

OBEROI AMARVILAS

A testament to love, new and old, this magnificent hotel offers a window (literally) to one of the new seven wonders of the world.

YEAR ESTABLISHED: **2000** NUMBER OF ROOMS: **102** FAMOUS FEATURE: **Taj Mahal view**
WHEN TO GO: **September–March**

At first glimpse, the Taj Mahal is extraordinary, but as you get closer, it exceeds expectations. It's bigger than you think and almost glows, with intricate designs etched into the white marble. It has been called the world's greatest monument to love: In 1631, the ruler of the Mughal Empire lost his favorite wife after she gave birth to their 14th child. This tomb, where they now both lay at rest, is an eternal shrine to their love.

Almost as impressive is Oberoi Amarvilas, where all rooms and suites (more than 100) have clear views of the Taj Mahal, as well as butler service. Built to reflect the grandeur of the mausoleum, the architecture is palatial—think marble everywhere, crafted by more than 600 artisans. Even the swimming pool was dug on a deeper level to avoid interfering with the views of the Taj Mahal.

Built from the ground up in 2000, the Oberoi Amarvilas has no deep-rooted history to reveal, though a long list of well-known names has already stayed here, usually in the 3,550-square-foot (330 m^2) Kohinoor Suite. More than just views make this a celebrity-worthy escape: Here, your window is a portal to a kind of explorer's magic that doesn't exist in everyday life. If you're not staying, book lunch or dinner at one of the hotel's restaurants (and watch out for the monkeys who might try to steal your food).

OPPOSITE: **The Taj Mahal can be seen right from your room at the Oberoi Amarvilas.**

JODHPUR, INDIA

TAJ UMAID BHAWAN PALACE

Get the royal treatment at this grand hotel, also a private palatial residence.

YEAR ESTABLISHED: **1943** NUMBER OF ROOMS: **70 (for guests); 347 in total** FAMOUS FEATURE: **Royal residences**
WHEN TO GO: **September–March**

Stay at the Taj Umaid Bhawan Palace to experience life as a maharaja (Indian royalty). This grand hotel in the Indian state of Rajasthan is also one of the world's largest private residences, still home to Gaj Singh (the beloved Bapji to locals), the grandson of the palace's namesake, Maharaja Umaid Singh. In 1971, Gaj Singh II decided to convert parts of the 347-room palace into a hotel to help maintain it; in 2005, the Taj group joined to manage the hotel. Today, guests have 70 art deco–style rooms to enjoy, including the grand Maharaja and Maharani Suites, former private royal bedrooms. It's also where Priyanka Chopra and Nick Jonas had their glorious wedding ceremony. Lucky visitors might just encounter Bapji while enjoying high tea, overlooking the perfectly manicured lawns where peacocks appear daily.

For Indians, the Taj brand represents more than just a hotel chain: "The Taj is a symbol of national pride," says Divia Thani, global editorial director of *Condé Nast Traveller* and a Mumbai native. "It's a showcase of the culture and traditions of India—and of its innate hospitality."

The hotel itself is one of the major attractions in the city, along with the on-site museum and restaurants that nonguests can usually book in advance. But Jodphur—known as the Blue City for its iconic blue rooftops—is really about wandering through the streets of the old city and discovering gems like the restored stepwell, and new stores and cafés.

OPPOSITE: Flowers float in the spectacular spa pool at the Taj Umaid Bhawan Palace.

HONG KONG, CHINA

THE PENINSULA HONG KONG

High tea and even higher luxury are offered at this stalwart hotel in the heart of ever changing Hong Kong.

YEAR ESTABLISHED: **1928** NUMBER OF ROOMS: **300** FAMOUS FEATURE: **Rolls-Royce fleet**
WHEN TO GO: **March–April or October–November**

"Having lived for almost 40 years in Hong Kong, the one constant—amid the sometimes tumultuous changes—is The Peninsula hotel," says Gerald Hatherly, an executive director at Abercrombie & Kent. "There may be flashier and what may be called 'flavor of the month' hotels, but there will always be The Peninsula with its elegance, Old World charm, and quaint traditions. It reassures Hong Kongers that though the future can seem unclear, The Peninsula remains, as it always has been, Hong Kong's finest hotel experience. Who doesn't love a Rolls-Royce transfer?"

Yes, The Peninsula Hong Kong has a fleet of 14 Rolls-Royces, painted in a signature emerald green—plus one vintage Rolls-Royce from 1934—to pick you up from the airport, as well as a helipad on the roof. Fitting to its Roaring Twenties beginnings, the Peninsula pages' white suits, inspired by Victorian-era military uniforms, remain unchanged. But the brand's first and flagship property continues to find ways to meld the future with its glamorous past.

Some of the most beloved hotel traditions have become synonymous with Hong Kong culture, most famously the afternoon tea. The Peninsula was the first hotel in the city to serve it. The scone recipe has remained the same for decades, and the brew is served from aged silver teapots. But each year, the hotel creates fun and new interpretations of the tea experience. Check the latest menu (which always includes scones) ahead of your visit.

OPPOSITE: **Travel in style with The Peninsula Hong Kong's fleet of Rolls-Royces.**

THE PENINSULA
THE PENINSULA
THE PENINSULA
THE PENINSULA
THE PENINSULA
THE PENINSULA

SHANGHAI, CHINA

WALDORF ASTORIA SHANGHAI ON THE BUND

Melding history with modernity, this former men's club is now a must-stay option for all on Shanghai's riverfront.

YEAR ESTABLISHED: **2010** NUMBER OF ROOMS: **252** FAMOUS FEATURE: **Long Bar**
WHEN TO GO: **March–April or October–November**

Perfectly positioned on Shanghai's historic Bund riverfront, this Waldorf Astoria property carefully combines the Shanghais of past and present. The original building, dating back to 1910, housed the Shanghai Club, an exclusive club for men frequented by famous literati, including W. Somerset Maugham and Noel Coward. The club operated in the 1920s and '30s, when Shanghai was called the "Paris of the East." Its Long Bar, which opened in 1911, was famous for being the world's longest at the time.

Fast-forward to 2010 when the Waldorf Astoria group opened Shanghai on the Bund. Housed within two buildings, the hotel combines Shanghai's futuristic promise with a taste of its legacy. The Heritage Building has more traditionally styled rooms. The new building, with more sleek and modern rooms, is called the Waldorf Towers, with views of glittering, neon Pudong across the Huangpu River. "Together they make for a hotel that has something for everyone," says Gerald Hatherly, an executive director at Abercrombie & Kent. "The service is warm and attentive, the breakfast buffet is Shanghai's best, and for anyone who lives for good Shanghai cuisine, its Chinese restaurant sets the standard for Shanghai hotels."

The original Long Bar design—dark and sexy—has been re-created down to every last detail. Today, it is one of the world's great hotel bars, with a list of drinks on the menu numbering in the hundreds.

ALTERNATE STAY

Built at the end of the Roaring Twenties, the Peace Hotel was Shanghai's grande dame. Today, this jazz-age, art deco landmark has been painstakingly restored to its original glory as the Fairmont Peace Hotel. The hotel offers Saturday Tea Dances, with professional ballroom instructors on hand to teach willing participants.

OPPOSITE: **With its high ceilings and columns, the Waldorf Astoria Shanghai on the Bund's reception area feels quite grand.**

BHUTAN

SIX SENSES BHUTAN

In a country that prides itself on sustainability and hospitality, these five properties stand above in honoring Bhutanese culture.

YEAR ESTABLISHED: **2018** NUMBER OF ROOMS: **Varies by location** FAMOUS FEATURE: **Cultural connection**
WHEN TO GO: **March–May or September–November**

Bhutan's vision of tourism has remained the same since it opened to the world in 1974: high value, low impact. Every visitor who comes into the kingdom pays a daily sustainability development fee that is funneled back into social projects, free health care, education, tourism, road infrastructure, and more. The result of a higher price tag for the privilege to enter the country: a well-preserved culture with little Western influence and one of the very few carbon-negative countries in the world.

Guests who visit are required to go through a local operator or a hotel like Six Senses. With five properties spread between the western and central Himalayan valleys of the kingdom, Six Senses has wellness at its core. The hotels here have the most extensive facilities in the kingdom, with heated swimming pools, saunas, yoga classes, and more. And under the pioneering leadership of longtime CEO Neil Jacobs, they have led the way in sustainable hospitality, long before it was expected.

Seventy percent of visitors to Bhutan do the "three-valley experience" across seven or eight nights. The three most popular valleys are Thimphu, Punakha, and Paro.

To see all five valleys and all five Six Senses properties, a minimum of 10 nights is recommended.

OPPOSITE: Six Senses Thimphu's infinity pond mirrors the surrounding jagged peaks.

PAGES 300–301: Find a luxurious, cabin-like retreat in the suites at Six Senses Paro.

Six Senses Thimphu, the "palace in the sky" at 8,695 feet (2,650 m) up in the Thimphu Valley. Often the first stop on a tour of Bhutan, it offers magnificent views over the capital city and one of the tallest seated Buddhas in the world.

Six Senses Punakha is located in a lush farming valley. The hotel's design is rustic chic, inspired by the surrounding rice fields. Guests hike to local monasteries and can enjoy riverside sunsets looking at the majestic Punakha Dzong across the way.

Six Senses Paro is the highlight of almost everyone's trip. You can't go to Bhutan without taking the hike to the famous Tiger's Nest, the 17th-century monastery built into the side of a cliff.

The remaining two Six Senses hotels take you back in time. Surrounded by serene, beautiful nature, **Six Senses Gangtey** is an intimate lodge known for its bird-watching, especially black-necked cranes. Meanwhile, **Six Senses Bumthang** is in one of Bhutan's spiritual centers.

It is an honor to be a part of this sustainable vision of hospitality, to counter negative impact while maximizing culture and connection. No wonder Bhutan consistently measures high on happiness levels.

AFTER CHECK-IN

The Bhutanese love spicy food. Try their national dish, *ema datshi,* or chili covered with melted cheese. Or a refreshing cucumber salad with chili and cilantro. Order a plate of *momos* (dumplings), usually accompanied by *ezay,* a very spicy Bhutanese condiment.

MALDIVES

BAROS MALDIVES

In a sea of overwater bungalows, this hotel stands above the rest with its deep-rooted connection to the local community.

YEAR ESTABLISHED: **1973** NUMBER OF ROOMS: **75** FAMOUS FEATURE: **Overwater bungalows**
WHEN TO GO: **November–April**

With more than 1,000 islands in the Indian Ocean, the Maldives satisfies travel dreams of a coconut-loaded tropical paradise with spectacular reefs for diving. But better go soon, as rising sea levels are threatening to envelop the low-lying chain. To counteract that threat, some of the most incredible hotels in the world are balancing sustainability and hospitality—and employing thousands of Maldivian locals.

At Baros, the house reef is considered to be one of the healthiest in the islands. The hotel opened in 1973 and has evolved from simple beach huts to a Maldivian icon while staying true to its local DNA. Maldivian Ibrahim Umar Maniku took over the resort decades ago, a rarity with so many international chains setting up shop on the archipelago. This is the quintessential Maldives hotel, with overwater bungalows and lush shades of green and blue everywhere. Suspended in the sea off a jetty, like a lampshade, the Lighthouse restaurant is more than worthwhile: The food celebrates Maldivian culture with strong flavors, curries, and fish.

Baros is less than 30 minutes from Velana International Airport via quick speedboat. No kids under eight years old are allowed. Maniku, who passed away in 2020, opened showstopper Milaidhoo in 2016, also close to Malé.

OPPOSITE: Guests can sleep soundly atop the beautiful blue ocean in villas at the Baros Maldives.

ASIA & THE MIDDLE EAST

BONUS STAYS

CAMBODIA

Raffles Hotel Le Royal, *Phnom Penh*

Combine a visit to Siem Riep and Angkor Wat with a couple nights in Phnom Penh staying at this landmark property. Open since 1929, it has hosted the likes of Charles de Gaulle and Jacqueline Kennedy, who have suites named after them. Sip a cocktail at the Elephant Bar, which has Cambodia's largest gin collection, cool off under the frangipani trees shading the pool, and enjoy Parisian-inspired food at Le Phnom 1929 or Khmer cuisine at Restaurant Le Royal.

CHINA

Aman at the Summer Palace, *Beijing*

Located 40 minutes from the center of Beijing, this Aman is adjacent to one of the city's most popular attractions, the Summer Palace, which UNESCO calls a "masterpiece of Chinese landscape garden design." The hotel's decor is inspired by the Ming dynasty. Split your stay between here and a hotel in central Beijing.

Banyan Tree Ringha, *Shangri-La*

In the Yunnan Province of China (which borders Myanmar and is also known as Shangri-la), the Banyan Tree Ringha was built from Tibetan farmhouses. This is a comfortable base to explore the lesser traveled treasures of the region, including local temples and villages, a nearby national park for hiking and exploring, and panoramic views of the mountains.

The Upper House, *Hong Kong*

Designed by André Fu (who is also behind the recently added spa at Claridge's in London, page 54), the Upper House rises above the Pacific Place shopping and dining complex. Rooms here start on the 38th floor. Even the entry-level rooms are spacious; all have views of the city's harbor, skyscrapers, or green mountains.

INDIA

Oberoi Rajvilas and Oberoi Udaivilas, *Jaipur and Udaipur*

Oberoi Amarvilas (page 290) overlooks the Taj Mahal, one of the new seven wonders of the world. But you can round out a stay in India with visits to Oberoi Rajvilas in the Pink City of Jaipur (known for jewelry and shopping amid historic forts and palaces) and Oberoi Udaivilas in Udaipur, an extraordinary palace structure with reflecting pools and views to Rajasthan's Lake Pichola.

JAPAN

Janu Tokyo, *Tokyo*

Janu Tokyo is the flagship debut of

OPPOSITE: Enjoy poolside dining at the Oberoi Rajvilas in Jaipur, India.

PAGES 306–307: An intricate layout of domes and corridors makes up the beautiful five-star Oberoi Udaivilas in Udaipur.

Aman's new spin-off hotel brand. The vibe is Aman (serene, private; see Amangiri, page 212), but the location in purpose-built Azabudai Hills is future-forward, with new retail, dining, and office spaces. The spa and wellness center houses Tokyo's largest gym. Janu will expand across the globe in the coming years.

The Ritz-Carlton Kyoto, *Kyoto*
Considered to be one of the best Ritz-Carlton properties in the world, not just Japan, this 134-room riverside hotel is inspired by the country's *ryokans,* or traditional inns. Dine at Michelin-starred Mizuki for Japanese cuisine, alongside Italian and French outlets.

Trunk (Hotel), *Tokyo*
Overlooking Tokyo's Yoyogi Park (which played host to many Olympic events in 1964), the newest location of Trunk Hotels—owned by Tokyo-native Yoshitaka Nojiri—plays to all five of its proclaimed pillars: environment, local first, diversity, health, and culture. The hotel feels like a place where Japan meets Scandinavia. The sixth-floor rooftop pool is open to guests only.

OMAN

The Chedi Muscat, *Muscat*
The Chedi operates sleek, peaceful Asian-inspired hotels across the Middle East (plus one in Andermatt, Switzerland). This beachfront property was a game changer for Oman. The hotel

ABOVE: **Vibrant mosaics from SICIS of Italy adorn the lobby walls of the opulent Reverie Saigon hotel in Vietnam.**

OPPOSITE: **Enjoy a steaming bowl of noodles and fresh seafood at the Chedi Muscat in Oman.**

offers fantastic dining options and is close to the airport for a quick transition into classic Omani relaxation.

UNITED ARAB EMIRATES

Madinat Jumeirah, *Dubai*

The Madinat Jumeirah is a feast for the senses. It's massive, with nearly 50 restaurants and bars on-site, a canal, two miles (3.2 km) of beach, a shopping complex called Souk Madinat, and multiple properties within. A favorite is Al Qasr, resembling an Arabian palace with striking marble and tiles, as well as huge displays of fresh flowers and fountains. And as is appropriate in Dubai, find views of the city's iconic Burj al Arab hotel from many vantage points.

VIETNAM

The Reverie Saigon, *Ho Chi Minh City*

Everything at the Reverie Saigon is opulent and glittering, with panoramic city views from rooms starting on the 27th floor. It's a visual sensation starting with the soaring lobby and its plush Italian fabrics, silks, marble, and gold. And yet the food, service, and history just outside the front door are distinctly Vietnamese.

PART FIVE

AFRICA

The tents of Angama Safari Camp (page 322), deep in the Masai Mara, glow in the evening light.

MARRAKECH, MOROCCO

LA MAMOUNIA

With a focus on Moroccan traditions, this glamorous hotel offers hospitality and history in a picture-perfect setting.

YEAR ESTABLISHED: 1929 **NUMBER OF ROOMS: 135** **FAMOUS FEATURE: Breakfast at Le Pavillon de la Piscine** **WHEN TO GO: March–May or September–November**

If you are researching the world's greatest hotels, Winston Churchill's name might keep popping up. He stayed at *a lot* of iconic properties, but one of his go-tos was La Mamounia, where he spent his winters. He called it the "most lovely spot in the whole world."

It's hard to argue with the prime minister's point. This property is deeply glamorous and romantic, a mini world of its own just steps away from the labyrinth of one of the world's largest *souks,* or markets.

"La Mamounia is synonymous with the magic of Marrakech," says frequent guest Melanie Brandman, who once welcomed 80 friends to the hotel for a party. "There is nothing more intoxicating than being ensconced in this extraordinary hotel or more romantic than being awakened in the morning by a chorus of birdsong and the view of the Atlas Mountains."

Alfred Hitchcock's 1956 thriller *The Man Who Knew Too Much* starred Doris Day and Jimmy Stewart as a couple staying at the hotel. The film sets the scene well: The intriguing and chaotic vibe of the city and the mystique of the hotel itself feel unchanged. Watch it before you visit; they filmed throughout the hotel and in the souk.

Upon arrival, guests are handed glasses of homemade almond milk and fresh dates, a perfect starter for a deliciously Moroccan visit. Long beloved (and photographed) for its Moorish meets art deco decor, the hotel has ornate tiles, layers of texture, and deep jewel tones of royal blue, lush purple, and vibrant reds throughout. There are many intimate corners to discover,

ALTERNATE STAY

For those looking for a classic, low-key *riad* (a traditional house built around a central courtyard), consider a stay at Riad Joya, co-owned by longtime Italian hotelier Marco Novella. With just seven rooms, it offers understated luxury in the middle of the medina.

OPPOSITE: Serve yourself at La Mamounia's decadent breakfast buffet.

ABOVE: **The timeless exterior of La Mamounia, one of Marrakech's finest stays**

OPPOSITE: **Al Mamoun Suite, adorned with antiques and paintings from around the world, is one of La Mamounia's most impressive offerings.**

from smaller courtyards to the cozy seating in the decades-old restaurant, Le Marocain.

Guests often linger over breakfast, which is a lavish buffet enjoyed at poolside tables at Le Pavillon de la Piscine, framed by the hotel's pink-and-green exterior and towering palm trees. Another daily ritual: a walk through the 17 acres (7 ha) of former royal gardens scented by florals and citrus.

The best rooms overlook these gardens, which give a sense of magic when lit at night. All have marble bathrooms, hammam-like showers, intricately carved arches, and more colorful tiles.

After recent renovations, some celebrity chefs and partners have been brought into the dining experiences. But the historic magic remains. In Moroccan Arabic, La Mamounia means "safe haven"—a feeling that follows you from check-in to checkout.

ASWAN & LUXOR, EGYPT

OLD CATARACT ASWAN & WINTER PALACE LUXOR

These hotels are inspired oases among Egypt's timeless relics.

YEAR ESTABLISHED: **1899 (Aswan); 1907 (Luxor)** NUMBER OF ROOMS: **220 (Aswan); 92 (Luxor)**
FAMOUS FEATURE: **High tea** WHEN TO GO: **October–April**

In *The Innocents Abroad,* Mark Twain writes of the Great Sphinx of Giza, "It was stone, but it seemed sentient ... It was gazing out over the ocean of Time—over lines of century-waves." When you see Egypt's ancient temples and relics in all their glory for yourself, you cannot help but think that these icons are alive, and have been for all eternity, encased in stone and watching over each generation that travels to see them.

Cairo and Giza are the natural starting points for a trip to Egypt—especially with the long-awaited opening of the Grand Egyptian Museum—but the best trip includes a leisurely drift down the Nile River past its desert-lush riverbanks. The odyssey allows you to travel back in time to some of the most jaw-dropping and well-preserved sites, tombs, and temples in the world. Many of these treasures are concentrated on the stretch of river between Luxor and Aswan, and in each city, you can visit two of the best hotels in Egypt for dinner or a stay: the Old Cataract Aswan and the Winter Palace Luxor, both under the Sofitel hotel umbrella.

"Egyptians feel glory and pride with these Victorian-era historical palaces," says Salwa Ahmed Abdelfattah, one of Egypt's top tour guides.

ALTERNATE STAY

When in Giza, book lunch or a stay at the historic Mena House hotel (now part of Marriott) before you visit the pyramids. Enjoy prime pyramid views and a sense of humor with your food—if your dish comes with rice, it arrives in the shape of a pyramid.

OPPOSITE: A view of the lavish, five-star Old Cataract Aswan

PAGES 318–319: Live like royalty in the Opera Suite at the Winter Palace Luxor.

To get a taste of that palatial history, watch the 1978 version of *Death on the Nile,* based on Agatha Christie's best-selling novel. Much of it was filmed at the **Old Cataract Aswan,** with its signature burnt sienna and white-lined exterior, situated on the curves of the Nile with evocative views of hundreds of palm trees, proud *felucca* sailboats, brown Nubian desert hills, and the striking contrast of tropical blue hotel pools. Enjoy high tea, cocktails, or a meal on the beautiful terraces.

The **Winter Palace Luxor,** however, is where Egypt meets Beverly Hills. A deeply romantic hotel, it shows off with royal gardens, a grand porte cochere entrance, and sunlit windows throughout. Built in the 19th century, it was officially launched as the Winter Palace Hotel in 1907. And though *Death on the Nile* was filmed at the Old Cataract, Agatha Christie herself sat on the Nile Terrace here writing the manuscript, inspired by the river views.

"As Egyptians, we feel totally nostalgic here, and every corner has a story," says Abdelfattah. "The last king of Egypt, Farouk, always stayed here." Farouk, like today's guests, enjoyed the hotel's beloved afternoon tea ritual in the Victorian

AFTER CHECK-IN

In Aswan, the must-see site is the Temple of Isis at Philae, honoring the goddess of maternity and love. "It was dismantled into 47,000 pieces to be moved and saved before the Aswan High Dam was completed in 1970," says Salwa Ahmed Abdelfattah.

ABOVE: A relief of Queen Nefertari from her tomb in the Valley of the Queens in Luxor, Egypt

OPPOSITE: A guest enjoys afternoon tea with a view from the Terrace restaurant at the Old Cataract Aswan.

Lounge, a tradition its many British guests brought over. Not without significance, it was here that British archaeologist and Egyptologist Howard Carter announced he had found King Tut's tomb in 1922. Quickly, the world press descended upon Luxor while Carter continued to post news and updates about the discovery in the hotel's public spaces. The exterior remains almost exactly as it would have been during Carter's time.

In Luxor, the top sightseeing highlights are in the Valleys of the Kings and Queens. But the greatest of all is Queen Nefertari's tomb. Words cannot express the awe of its vivid, pristine colors, which are more than 3,200 years old. (Book your visit early. A limited number of visitors are allowed each day, with a high ticket price.)

It is a testament to the power and ingenuity of the Egyptians that everything here feels completely timeless.

MASAI MARA, KENYA

ANGAMA MARA

Find yourself on a movie set in this Out of Africa *destination that offers a prime safari experience.*

YEAR ESTABLISHED: **2015** NUMBER OF ROOMS: **15** FAMOUS FEATURE: **Masai Mara views**
WHEN TO GO: **July–September**

Angama Mara is known for its heart-stopping, panoramic views across Kenya's Masai Mara. The vistas feel straight out of the movie *Out of Africa*—because it actually is. Many scenes of the classic film, which premiered in 1985, were made at this site. "You know you are truly alive when you are living among lions," writes author Karen Blixen, who was played by Meryl Streep in the movie.

Among the lions and the rest of Africa's big five—leopards, rhinos, Cape buffalo, and elephants—Angama Mara is more than alive. When it opened in 2015, this lodge quickly established itself as one of the best in East Africa, thanks to owners Steve and Nicky Fitzgerald, safari industry legends. Nicky, in particular, has always been a delightful storyteller. Though Steve passed away in 2017 and Nicky retired from full-time work in 2022, daughter Kate Boyd is still involved in the day-to-day, and the lodge carries on the Fitzgerald passion and leadership to create incredible African travel experiences and to support local communities in concrete ways.

Angama Mara has expanded to include Angama Safari Camp, a movable camp set up for private groups of up to eight, which Nicky says captures the "glorious adventure of the golden age of the African safari." As well, the 10-room Angama Amboseli sits in the Kimana Sanctuary, a 5,700-acre (2,307 ha) reserve owned by hundreds of Maasai families and offering the backdrop of Kilimanjaro in Tanzania.

ALTERNATE STAY

Mara Plains Camp, located in the Olare Motorogi Conservancy on the northern border of the Masai Mara, is owned by the Great Plains Foundation and Beverly and Dereck Joubert (see Duba Plains and Zarafa Camps in Botswana, page 348). The National Geographic Explorers are two trusted and seasoned veterans who know what they want in terms of location, style, wildlife, conservation, and experience.

OPPOSITE: Float over the Masai Mara in a hot-air balloon and spot wildlife from above.

LEWA WILDLIFE CONSERVANCY, KENYA

SIRIKOI LODGE

A model in conservation, this lodge has been a part of a rhino repopulation effort and also offers private safari experiences.

YEAR ESTABLISHED: 2000 **NUMBER OF ROOMS: Six** **FAMOUS FEATURE: Luxury tents**
WHEN TO GO: July–September

Sirikoi Lodge is surrounded by 68,000 acres (27,519 ha) of the Lewa Wildlife Conservancy, a UNESCO World Heritage site and one of the most successful privately owned and family-driven models of conservation in Africa.

At the heart of Sirikoi are the owners and the rhinos, according to Phoebe Weinberg, owner of Greatways Travel in Michigan and an Africa travel expert who has traveled to the continent more than 80 times. "Seeing the rhinos here is hugely important, because other than South Africa, you can just about forget about it," she says.

Beginning with just 15 black rhinos in 1984, the population has grown much higher (the exact number is kept secret) today thanks to the conservancy's efforts, which include behind-the-scenes educational opportunities for guests.

"I can't tell you how magical it is at Sirikoi," says Weinberg. "Lewa was formed back in the 1980s by five generational Kenyan families, among them the Roberts and Dyer families. There is so much history. It's the real Kenya. It's sitting in their lounge with all the pictures and listening to the stories. You can't touch that with a new property."

The owners of the Lewa Wildlife Conservancy, including the Robertses, have close ties with the British royal family. In fact, Prince William proposed to Kate Middleton within the conservancy.

Sirikoi is intimate, with just a few accommodation options. For families, the best choice is a three-bedroom house or the two-bedroom cottage.

OPPOSITE: A woman prepares the table for a meal at Sirikoi, known for fresh, elegant home-style cooking.

PAGES 326–327: Enjoy quiet evenings in the Lewa Wildlife Conservancy inside Sirikoi's luxury tented rooms.

There are also four luxury tents, each with private decks.

Aside from the success with rhinos, Sirikoi maintains vigorous sustainable travel practices. Among them, it runs on 100 percent solar power and has an on-site organic vegetable garden, and all proceeds from spa treatments are donated to local schools and orphanages.

Though many of our most iconic African safari images come from the Masai Mara in Kenya—famous pictures of zebras and wildebeests crossing the Mara River abound—Lewa is conversely located at the foot of Mount Kenya. A combination stay between the Mara (Angama Mara, page 322) and the Lewa Wildlife Conservancy is an ideal way to see Kenya, with very different topography and fewer safari vehicles to compete with.

"Especially during migration, it's getting more and more crowded in the Masai Mara," says Weinberg. "Last time I was there, I counted 92 vehicles. There are more than 80 camps in the Mara and surrounding conservancies; there are fewer than 10 in the Lewa. And Sirikoi is the premier property."

ALTERNATE STAY

Other wonderful lodge options within the Lewa Wildlife Conservancy also support the larger mission. Standouts include two Elewana properties—Kifaru House and Lewa Safari Camp—as well as Lewa Wilderness, owned by the Craig family, who set aside 5,000 acres (2,023 ha) of their ranch in 1983 to help protect the black rhino.

GRUMETI GAME RESERVE, TANZANIA

SINGITA LODGES

Find a sense of wholeness at this family-run lodge just outside Serengeti National Park.

YEAR ESTABLISHED: **1993** NUMBER OF ROOMS: **Multiple camps, rooms vary** FAMOUS FEATURE: **Grumeti Fund**
WHEN TO GO: **Year-round**

Singita originates from South Africa in the region of the Shangaan people, where their word *masingita* means "miracle." Indeed, what Singita has achieved, with arguably the most esteemed properties in Africa, does feel miraculous.

The through line of Singita's properties across Africa is its commitment to a 100-year purpose to conserve and protect large areas of Africa's natural world. Every aspect—the people, design, food, energy, game drives, and activities—reflects this purpose.

Founder Luke Bailes inherited a South African farmstead purchased by his grandfather in 1923. Today, that former family home is Singita Castleton, one of numerous Singita lodges, camps, and villas found throughout South Africa, Tanzania, Zimbabwe, and Rwanda. "If I could sum it up, Singita is all about the way it makes you feel, that deep feeling you receive on the African continent," says Jo Bailes, Luke's son and Singita's CEO.

Each Singita lodge could stand alone as an entry in this book. But the story of Singita Grumeti in Tanzania is remarkable. It has a total of seven properties: the manor-style **Sasakwa Lodge;** the chic and contemporary **Faru Faru Lodge; Sabora** and **Mara River tented camps; Explore mobile tented camp;** and exclusive villas, **Serengeti House** and **Milele.** (Many guests stay at two or three on a visit.) "A lot of African lodges take inspiration from the past," Jo Bailes says. "We're taking inspiration from the future, with deep African influence and a profound sense of place in the design."

BRING IT HOME

Bring a piece of Singita, and Africa, home through its online shop, which sells furniture, jewelry, home decor, clothing, and more—all supporting local artisans and makers. One recent collaboration? Beautiful dresses from famous South African designer Thebe Magugu.

OPPOSITE: Become immersed in the natural beauty of Tanzania at the Sabora Tented Camp.

ABOVE: **Singita Serengeti House offers dining experiences out in the bush.**

OPPOSITE: **A family of cheetahs sits at the Singita Grumeti Game Reserve.**

PAGES 332–333: **The secluded location of the Hillside Suite at Singita Sasakwa Lodge makes it the perfect private retreat for two.**

The Singita Grumeti properties sit on the 350,000-acre (141,640 ha) Grumeti Game Reserve, adjacent to Serengeti National Park, a critical corridor for the great wildebeest migration and known for excellent lion sightings.

The lodges here are inextricably linked to the Grumeti Fund, the nonprofit conservation entity that Singita has been the tourism partner of since 2005, helping to ensure sustainable financial support and working with local communities. Singita employs more than 800 people. Tanzania's population is growing at a rapid rate, and managing the human-wildlife conflict is a huge part of the work done by the Grumeti Fund. Among their other projects, the Grumeti Fund and Singita support anti-poaching scouts with state-of-the-art digital radios, a specialist canine unit, tracker training programs, scholarships for local students, the clearance of "alien" vegetation, and water conservation.

Tanzania used to be a "three-month destination," visited only around the wildebeest migration in June, July, and August. In the early 1990s, the eco-

system was overgrazed and degraded, and much of the game had been poached or hunted. The incredible work by Singita and the Grumeti Fund has allowed for a thriving ecosystem, increased wildlife numbers (including 1,200 elephants, grown from a dwindling population of 350), and reasons to visit year-round.

Singita's wellness approach focuses on mental, physical, and emotional wholeness. "One of our fundamental pillars is that we ensure you have an exclusive time in the bush, on your own," Bailes says. "Time alone in the wilderness is where the deep change is made within you."

A stay at Singita is life-changing, bringing you to a place where you feel both powerful and insignificant, connected to humanity and the wilderness.

"Many of these cultures [in Africa] have deep and soulful philosophies of life that we should learn and take with us," says Bailes, "the way they look after and care for nature and each other as part of a larger ecosystem."

AFTER CHECK-IN

Watch out for African wild dogs, one of the world's most endangered species and Jo Bailes's favorite to spot. "They're so fast and quick—they're almost there and nowhere at the same time," he says. "They're pack animals. The strong look after the weak, the old after the young. Most predators fight when they eat but not wild dogs, as it's all about sharing and giving."

SOUTH AFRICA

THE ROYAL PORTFOLIO

Full of personality and vibrancy, these one-of-a-kind lodges all offer a different view of South Africa.

YEAR ESTABLISHED: **1999** NUMBER OF ROOMS: **Varies by location** FAMOUS FEATURE: **Vibrant colors**
WHEN TO GO: **Year-round**

To experience the best of South Africa, follow a regal itinerary with a 10-day circuit of the Royal Portfolio's brilliant and groundbreaking hotels. On the grand tour, you'll safari at Royal Malewane; experience the urban buzz and art at The Silo in Cape Town; take in the coastal beauty at Birkenhead House; and imbibe in the food and wine of Franschhoek at La Residence.

"My mother wanted to share the beauty of South Africa with people," says Matt Biden, son of Phil and Liz Biden and CEO of the Royal Portfolio. Liz was a teacher before running and selling a fashion business. After one day of retirement, she decided to rent out a few rooms of the family's vacation home in Greater Kruger National Park to cover some costs. That one decision grew to become **Royal Malewane,** which opened in 1999 and now encompasses three lodge options—Malewane, Farmstead, and Waterside—on 35,000 acres (14,165 ha) of the Thornybush Nature Reserve, adjacent to Kruger National Park.

Next came **Birkenhead House,** which was the family's beach house in Hermanus, an area known for excellent whale-watching. Less than an hour from Cape Town in the country's culinary and wine region is **La Residence,** which boasts gilded mirrors and sculptures, chandeliers from India, and dramatic colors throughout. "It's not maximalism," says travel writer Becca Hensley. "It's more a kind of nouveau baroque, postmodernist madness."

AFTER CHECK-IN

Forage and feast: At Birkenhead House, take surf lessons with the general manager, then meet the chef in your wet suit to pick mussels off the rocks for that evening's dinner. Matt Biden loves the seafood platter here, another must-try.

OPPOSITE: Through the funky windows of a one-bedroom penthouse suite in The Silo, enjoy panoramic views of Cape Town.

PAGES 336–337: Guests on a safari enjoy an up close encounter with an elephant.

LAND CRUISER
ROYAL MALEWANE

In 2017, **The Silo,** a striking modern marvel in Cape Town, opened in a century-old grain silo, showcasing the concrete and steel that has been there since the 1920s. Defining elements include the black-and-white-striped bathrooms and the huge panoramic windows, designed with 56 individual panels of glass on each one. From the outside, they almost appear to be in motion, expanding from inside. Equally important are the links to the booming contemporary African art scene. The Silo shares its space with the Zeitz Museum of Contemporary Art, and an on-site art concierge helps guests tour the hotel's 350-plus pieces, starting in the guest rooms. Nonguests can reserve a spot at The Silo Rooftop for sunset Cape Town views.

All the properties also support projects relevant to their location through the Royal Portfolio Foundation. The Biden family has been helping the community for more than 35 years, long before their first hotel. Among the many projects are paying the headmistresses' salaries at underresourced schools and supporting a home for abused children. Every employee is expected to work twice a year at one of the projects, and the company also built the Conservation & Research Centre at Royal Malewane, with free bedrooms for visiting scientists.

WHILE YOU'RE THERE

In Cape Town, set on the slopes of Table Mountain, visit Kirstenbosch National Botanical Garden, one of the most otherworldly and beautiful gardens in the world.

TSWALU KALAHARI RESERVE, SOUTH AFRICA

TSWALU KALAHARI

In an arid climate with multiple options for accommodations, this collection of lodges offers the chance to see rarer species on safari.

YEAR ESTABLISHED: 1994 **NUMBER OF ROOMS:** 15 **FAMOUS FEATURE:** Pangolins **WHEN TO GO:** Year-round

Near the border of Botswana lies Tswalu Kalahari Reserve, 282,000 acres (114,000 ha) of malaria-free landscape within the Kalahari Desert. Tswalu is a leader in conservation, rewilding, and protection on farmland purchased by South Africa's Oppenheimer family.

Only about 30 guests at a time get to enjoy the vast reserve. The original Motse Safari Camp has nine suites and welcomes children of all ages, a rarity for African camps. For multigenerational families, the Tarkuni Homestead has a plunge pool and firepit, while Loapi Tented Camp offers safari-style glamping. You can also sleep outside under the stars on one of two Star Beds.

"Safari veterans *love* Tswalu," says Africa travel expert and owner of Fig Travel Co. Tiffany Figueiredo. "It is a unique green-Kalahari experience. It was already my favorite and upped its cool factor by opening a JAN outpost under a farmhouse in the middle of the desert." Chef Jan Hendrik van der Westhuizen earned his Michelin star in Nice, France, but opened this Kalahari location, his first restaurant in his home country of South Africa, in 2021. Tswalu also just opened six new ultraluxe tented suites that raise the bar on African wilderness glamping.

Owing to a semiarid landscape with extreme temperatures and microclimates, wildlife sightings differ from those on a typical safari. The Tswalu Foundation funds advanced research on ground pangolins, said to be the most trafficked mammal in the world, which can be spotted on game drives (though they are predominately nocturnal), along with other less observed species including aardvarks, brown hyenas, and bat-eared foxes.

OPPOSITE: Spend a cozy evening admiring the night sky at Tarkuni Homestead's firepit.

TANZANIA

MWIBA LODGE

One of the most significant safari lodges, this legendary property is known for its cultural connections and showstopping safaris.

YEAR ESTABLISHED: **2013** NUMBER OF ROOMS: **10** FAMOUS FEATURE: **Cultural engagement**
WHEN TO VISIT: **July–September**

Set on its own private 130,000-acre (53,000 ha) reserve, Mwiba Lodge, part of Legendary Expeditions, is an architectural feat built overlooking a water hole. Every room has its own private view to the watering hole, a gathering place for the wildlife you've come here for.

Due to its distinct topography, Mwiba's focus is on community and cultural engagement—a highlight for guests who thought they were coming here for the big five. Though an experience is not guaranteed, guests are often invited to walk with the Hadza hunter-gatherer tribe to watch and learn about their ancient traditions and ways of life. (For instance, they are immune to bee stings, and will use bare hands to take out fresh honeycomb.)

The wildlife, including elephants and hippos, is abundant. And it's not uncommon to find a giraffe at the end of your balcony while taking a bubble bath. You'll feel one with nature here as each of the 10 suites has a private deck and outdoor rain shower. The main lodge, which offers a spa and fitness center, has a pool that overlooks the area's natural springs—you'll see plenty of wildlife visiting there throughout your stay.

Many guests complete the "Legendary loop" by starting in Arusha at Legendary Lodge, a working coffee plantation and the perfect place to stop for a night before safari. Next is Mila Tented Camp, closest to the Grumeti, with its flat plains and cheetahs, before ending at Mwiba.

Legendary Expeditions protects more than 547,453 acres (221,546 ha) of land with significant anti-poaching and community support initiatives.

ALTERNATE STAY

Some guests choose to add Chem Chem Lodge, near Lake Manyara, to the "Legendary loop." The ecosystem and landscape here are different, a bit more tropical (with palm trees!). And the lodge has a big focus on birding. This formerly overfarmed, overpoached corridor has been brought back to life and is considered one of the most important on the continent now.

OPPOSITE: Enjoy safari views with a meal at the lodge's jacuzzi area.

SOUTH AFRICA

LONDOLOZI PRIVATE GAME RESERVE

A leader in safari conservation and sustainable tourism, Londolozi has played a large role in South Africa's history.

YEAR ESTABLISHED: **1926** NUMBER OF ROOMS: **Five camps, rooms vary** FAMOUS FEATURE: **Leopards**
WHEN TO GO: **Year-round**

"Londolozi is chockablock with leopards," says safari expert and owner of Fig Travel Co. Tiffany Figueiredo. Seeing the spotted big cat is a hallmark experience at Londolozi, the meaning of which comes from a Zulu word for "protector of all living things."

The reserve's owners, the Varty family, are true pioneers of conservation-focused safari camps and are passionately devoted to sustainable tourism. Located on a reserve bordering Kruger National Park, the accommodations consist of five separate camps, two of which allow children six and up.

As they developed the land in the 1970s, the Vartys wanted to show that wildlife tourism could be an economic driver as well as a healing force. Nelson Mandela spent several weeks at Londolozi, learning about the power of the safari industry to create opportunity and development.

As Mandela recalled: "I saw people of all races living in harmony amidst the beauty that Mother Nature offers. Londolozi represents a model of the dream I cherish for the future of nature preservation in our country."

Owner Dave Varty spent several days with Mandela. He showed the anti-apartheid activist Africa's big five for the first time and inspired conservation policies that Mandela would later implement as president.

OPPOSITE: On a safari drive, a vehicle stops to let guests watch two leopards in a tree.

RWANDA

WILDERNESS BISATE

Set near six dormant volcanoes, this lodge is a model in ecotourism and offers a chance for close encounters with gorillas.

YEAR ESTABLISHED: 2017 **NUMBER OF ROOMS:** Six **FAMOUS FEATURE:** Gorillas
WHEN TO GO: June–September or December–February

In the green northwest of Rwanda, the iconic mountain gorillas and endemic golden monkeys go about their daily lives. But safari opportunities here offer a chance to get close. "When you are within 10 meters of a gorilla, you make eye contact and it's absolutely fascinating," says Rob Baas, managing director of Wilderness Rwanda. "It's almost the same as a human—you can see what they're thinking at the moment and you wonder, What does he think of me?"

To see these gorillas is a trip of a lifetime, more so since Wilderness pioneered high-end tourism in the region (luxe competitors Singita Kwitonda and One&Only Gorilla's Nest followed). Prior to the lodge's opening in 2017, the land was purchased from local communities and a reforestation program began, with more than 85,000 indigenous trees planted. After the effort succeeded, the lodge was built almost adjacent to Volcanoes National Park, with views of six beautiful (and dormant) volcanoes. The lodge's six round villas were inspired by the design of the former King's Palace in Nyanza, with vibrant local details conceived by Rwandan designer Teta Isibo.

Just 20 minutes from the lodge is the entrance to the gorilla trek, where you begin the hike through the tropical forest. The majority of guests stay for three nights and do two gorilla treks. "The first trek is so emotional that

BEFORE CHECK-IN

Read Josh Ruxin's memoir, *A Thousand Hills to Heaven,* which chronicles how he and his wife, Alissa, moved to Rwanda in 2005 to fight poverty and create jobs for orphans of the country's genocide. In Kigali, visit their boutique hotel, the Retreat.

OPPOSITE: Take in the canopy views from Wilderness Bisate's luxurious lounge.

ABOVE: **Nest-like villas, tucked away in the rainforest canopy, overlook incredible views of the Rwandan wilderness.**

OPPOSITE: **Lucky trekkers might see baby gorillas hanging on to their mothers in the wild.**

people are very ready for a second one," Baas says. "Most people do the monkey trek as well, and enjoy visiting a community next to the property, which is really genuine and not set up."

Rwandan officials knew they couldn't have thousands of tourists and continue to maintain a sustainable wildlife ecosystem, so the country set a high-cost, low-impact model to protect the animals and environment.

In 2019, Wilderness opened their Magashi lodge in Akagera National Park. Says Baas: "After the [Rwandan] genocide, a lot of refugees came to the park and most of the animals were wiped out. African Parks [a nonprofit] asked us if we saw potential and we thought it was a beautiful conservation story." With just eight rooms and tented suites here, it's a hidden gem, as most safari seekers don't realize Rwanda offers more than gorillas. By the time of check-out, 60 to 70 percent of guests have seen all of the big five.

BOTSWANA

DUBA PLAINS & ZARAFA CAMPS

Spot the big five like National Geographic Explorers at these private lodges in a robust wildlife environment.

YEAR ESTABLISHED: **2017 (Duba Plains); 2008 (Zarafa)** NUMBER OF ROOMS: **Five (Duba Plains); five (Zarafa)**
FAMOUS FEATURE: **Extraordinary wildlife** WHEN TO GO: **April–August**

Documentary filmmakers, authors, conservationists, and National Geographic Explorers at large, Dereck and Beverly Joubert have dedicated their lives to saving the natural world and wildlife in Africa. Along with the National Geographic Society, they founded the Big Cats Initiative, which has funded more than 150 conservation projects across 28 countries. The Jouberts' luxury safari company, Great Plains Conservation, with camps in Botswana, Kenya, and Zimbabwe, exists to fund their conservation work through the Great Plains Foundation.

Botswana is one of Africa's least-crowded countries, with the flood season (May through September) giving way to the green season (October through March), and year-round extraordinary wildlife sightings. To experience the epitome of a safari in Botswana, where the Jouberts live, Duba Plains Camp and Zarafa (meaning "beloved one") Camp make an ideal combination.

Duba Plains Camp is in the heart of the Okavango Delta, in the private Duba Plains Reserve, renowned for its lion and buffalo populations, which are well documented in the Jouberts' 2006 film, *Relentless Enemies*. The camp's five suites are classic 1920s safari style with views to the floodplains.

Zarafa Camp is located on the 320,000-acre (129,500 ha) Selinda Reserve, with a romantic lantern light in each of its four rooms, plus the two-bedroom tented Dhow Suite, made entirely from reclaimed wood.

MEET UP

Guests can ask to learn about and experience the work of the Great Plains Foundation during their stay. Among the projects are Rhinos Without Borders, which funds the moves of endangered rhinos to Botswana, and Solar Mamas, which trains women to use solar power for electricity.

OPPOSITE: Zarafa Camp, located in the private Selinda Reserve, features spacious canvas tents, each with a lavish bedroom and a bathroom with a copper claw-foot tub.

AFRICA

BONUS STAYS

BOTSWANA

Jack's Camp, *Kalahari*

One of Africa's most beloved camps, Jack's Camp, which fully runs on solar power, underwent a full renovation in 2021, while retaining its safari glamour and Old World soul. It doubles as a mini natural history museum with the most incredible collection of fossils and artifacts for guests to enjoy. Named for Jack Bousfield, a safari pioneer who brought tourism to the Makgadikgadi Pan (a desert salt pan), Jack's Camp was opened by his son Ralph in 1993 and ensures that visitors will always want to come back.

KENYA

Giraffe Manor, *Nairobi*

Though it is a global sensation, this hotel manages to exceed expectations, allowing guests to get close to giraffes (and contribute to conservation efforts simply by staying) against the backdrop of a century-old manor house in Karen, a suburb of Nairobi. Owned by Kenyans Tanya and Mikey Carr-Hartley, it is the flagship property of the Safari Collection.

Kalepo Camp, *Samburu*

This exclusive-use tented camp is a beautiful jumping-off point to explore local culture (through the Samburu people) and wildlife, like the Reteti Elephant Sanctuary. "To me, Kalepo embodies the true spirit of Africa," says safari expert Stephanie Capuano, partner at &Three Collective. "The food, wine, design, and hospitality are remarkable, too."

Segera Retreat, *Nanyuki*

Owned by Jochen Zeitz, former CEO of Puma, Segera Retreat on the Laikipia Plateau in northern Kenya has pioneered conservation efforts in the region through the Zeitz Foundation. Accommodations are split between stand-alone structures, including the greenhouse, farmhouse, Segera House, garden villas, and more.

MADAGASCAR

Time + Tide Miavana, *Nosy Anko*

Now part of top safari-meets-beach itineraries, Miavana changed luxury tourism in Madagascar. You can arrive here only by helicopter, adding to the feeling of remote, intriguing seclusion. The owners planted more than 100,000 indigenous trees and created 14 villas using only natural and recycled materials. The coral reefs offer extraordinary diving.

MOROCCO

Dar Ahlam, *Skoura*

This 200-year-old restored casbah, or fortress, sits surrounded by almond and

OPPOSITE: During a stay at Shipwreck Lodge in Namibia, go on a sand-boarding adventure in the world's oldest desert: the Namib.

PAGES 352–353: Enjoy fine teas and treats inside the Persian tea tent at Jack's Camp in Botswana.

palm trees in the Moroccan desert. Dar Ahlam means "house of dreams," and the hotel truly is a dream realized for Frenchman Thierry Teyssier, who helped inform every design decision. He wanted a hotel based on guests' needs and desires rather than restrictions like set check-in and checkout times. With just 14 rooms, the hotel is a member of Small Luxury Hotels of the World.

NAMIBIA

andBeyond Sossusvlei Desert Lodge, *Sossusvlei*

Of the many andBeyond properties around the world, Sossusvlei Desert Lodge is a top option, located in the Namib Desert. Thanks to little light pollution, the lodge offers extraordinary stargazing. Take a unique desert safari, climb (and board down) some of the world's tallest dunes, or simply gaze up at the night sky from the lodge's pool.

Shipwreck Lodge, *Mowe Bay*

New hotels continue to open each year in Namibia, but Shipwreck Lodge in Skeleton Coast National Park was one of the originals. The hotel showcases the otherworldly and dramatic landscapes of the country. The distinctive cabin design—yes, it looks like a shipwreck—was inspired by stories of lost ships that line the nearby South Atlantic coast.

SOUTH AFRICA

Ellerman House, *Cape Town*

Ellerman House is completely spectacular. The hotel boasts a museum-quality

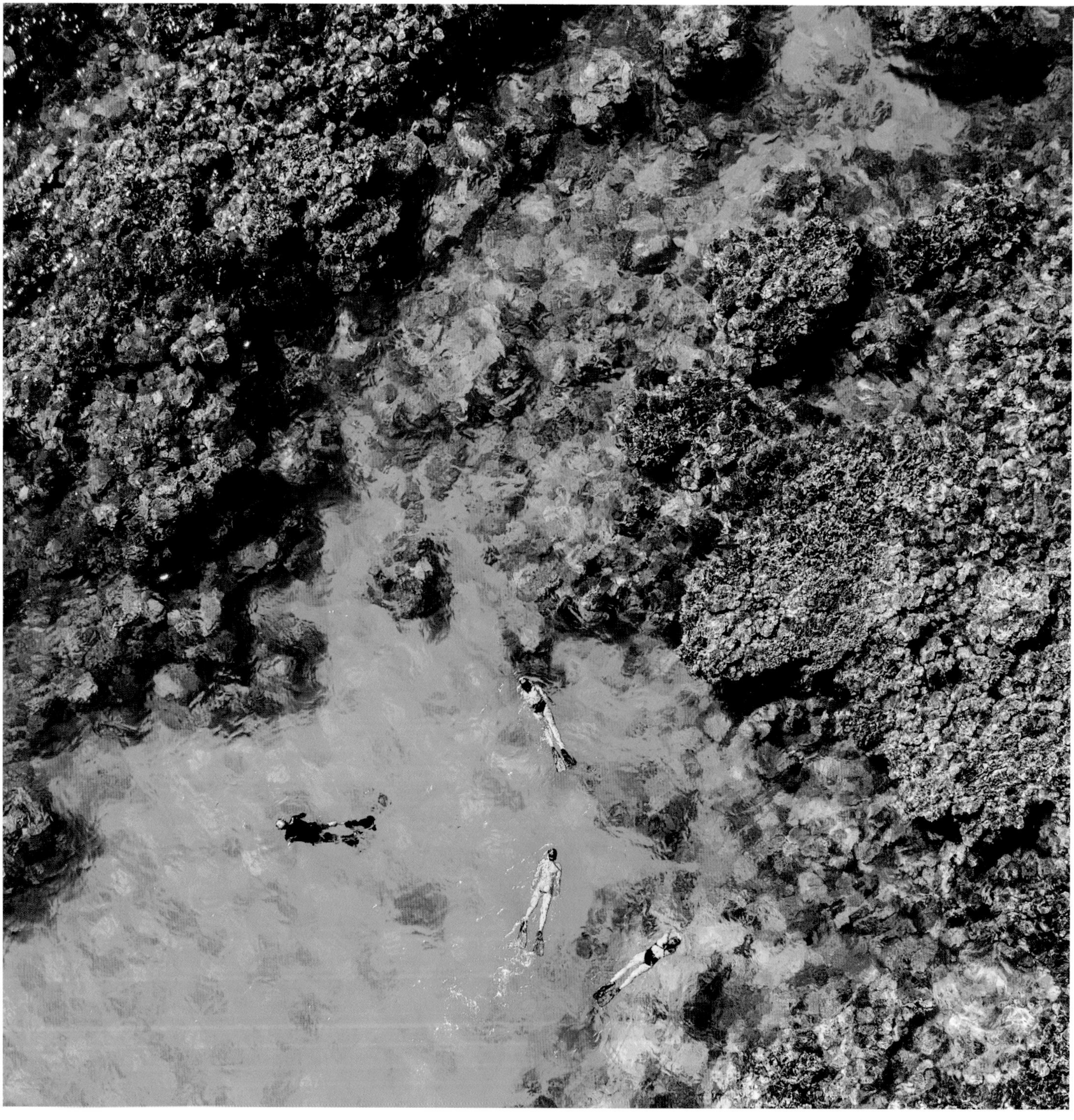

ABOVE: **The quiet, nature-filled grounds of Dar Ahlam lie on the edge of Morocco's desert.**

OPPOSITE: **Snorkel through a 37,066-acre (15,000 ha) marine protected area during a stay at Time + Tide Miavana in Madagascar.**

collection that stems from the passion of owner Paul Harris. Set on a cliffside in residential Bantry Bay, the Edwardian mansion has just 13 rooms and villas, terraced gardens surrounding the pool, and a primarily South African wine collection. On the terroir wall, guests are encouraged to touch and feel soil samples from more than 100 South African vineyards.

TANZANIA

Taasa Lodge, ***Serengeti***

Located just outside Serengeti National Park, Taasa Lodge is a family-friendly safari destination worthy of the trip to get here. With a concession from the government that allows off-roading, the lodge gets safari seekers as close to the big five as safely possible. Two game drives are offered each day, as well as night drives, a boma dinner, and a visit to a local Maasai tribe. The majority of the lodge staff are local Maasai and happily share their knowledge of the environment and animals with guests. You'll never find a welcome quite like the one you receive at Taasa—and you'll find yourself wanting to stay for all the little extras that add up to a once-in-a-lifetime trip.

PART SIX

OCEANIA

Try fresh, locally sourced farm-to-table dining at Wharekauhau on the North Island of New Zealand (page 358).

KAUHAU

NORTH ISLAND, NEW ZEALAND

WHAREKAUHAU LODGE

Remote and wild, this unique lodge lets you become one with nature—and sheep—through its one-of-a-kind experiences.

YEAR ESTABLISHED: 1980s **NUMBER OF ROOMS: 16** **FAMOUS FEATURE: Working sheep station tour**
WHEN TO GO: December–February or April–May

Set on a 3,000-acre (1,215 ha) estate of rolling woodlands and lakes and overlooking Palliser Bay at the southern tip of the North Island, Wharekauhau (pronounced forrie-COE-hoe) revolves around a large slate of experiential offerings.

Just more than five million people live in New Zealand, with around 26 million sheep. Suffice it to say, sheep have played an important role in the history and farming culture of the country. So it's no surprise that the signature experience here is a three-hour working sheep station tour.

But this stunning country estate, located a 90-minute drive from Wellington, is not all about the sheep. "This is one of the more remote and rugged corners of New Zealand, and it's exactly this location that makes it so special," says Sarah Farag, a director at Southern Crossings travel company. Guests can choose to explore by e-bike or ATV, visit a popular nearby seal colony and fishing village, go wine tasting, practice archery, and much more. Day guests also have many options, including a chef-led lunch and spa treatments.

At the end of the day, "you almost find yourself willing a late storm to roll in off the ocean," says Farag, "so you can see the waves churning and listen to the creaking and groaning of the pine trees, all while sipping on a rich Pinot Noir in front of your in-room fireplace."

OPPOSITE: Beneath the rugged Remutaka Range, Wharekauhau boasts 3,000 acres (1,215 ha) of private, natural grounds.

CHRISTCHURCH, NEW ZEALAND

OTAHUNA LODGE

Fresh food is on the menu at this historic Queen Anne home, which offers a taste of New Zealand's grand history.

YEAR ESTABLISHED: **1895** NUMBER OF ROOMS: **Seven** FAMOUS FEATURE: **Produce gardens**
WHEN TO GO: **December–February or April–May**

Set atop a small hill and surrounded by exceptional gardens and woodlands with views of the Canterbury Plains and Southern Alps in the distance, Otahuna Lodge may be small—it has just seven rooms—but it is most definitely grand, a historic showpiece of Queen Anne architecture with a white wood exterior and gabled roofs.

"Otahuna Lodge is without a doubt one of New Zealand's grandest homes," says Sarah Farag, a director at travel company Southern Crossings. "The stately mansion sits on the outskirts of the Garden City of Christchurch and boasts gardens of national significance. When the current owners bought it, the homestead was in ruins, but it has been meticulously restored and filled with fine art and luxurious antique furnishings."

A private home for more than 60 years, Otahuna was originally owned by Sir Heaton Rhodes, a popular figurehead in the community, and his family. The elegant Rhodes Suite, with a cozy Victorian fireplace, was the primary owners' bedroom and is named in his honor.

Today, Otahuna is a globally recognized destination for food lovers, who come for a dinner (and wine pairing) of a lifetime. The expansive gardens grow more than 175 different types of produce, including nuts and mushrooms in the potager (kitchen) garden; the Dutch garden is fragrant with lavender, pine, and more. Guests can forage with the amazing on-site chef to choose their own vegetables for dinner or take a cooking class. There are occasional class offerings for non-staying guests.

OPPOSITE: Otahuna Lodge, with its entrance featuring classic wooden archways and refined decor, is a lavish place to stay on the South Island.

SOUTH ISLAND, NEW ZEALAND

BLANKET BAY

Embark on an adventure of a lifetime at this trendsetting wilderness lodge less than an hour from Queenstown.

YEAR ESTABLISHED: **1999** NUMBER OF ROOMS: **13** FAMOUS FEATURE: **Helicopter tours**
WHEN TO GO: **December–February or April–May**

Blanket Bay is one of New Zealand's first luxury adventure lodges and remains a trendsetter and leader in the industry. That's a testament to the quality of the offerings and the unspoiled beauty of its surroundings. Here, the mountain ranges and waters are straight out of a J. R. R. Tolkien fantasy, Middle-earth come to life more than anywhere else in New Zealand.

Cozy alpine ski lodge meets New Zealand adventure at this welcoming retreat with gabled roofs and a mix of brick and timber. A 30-foot-high (9 m) Great Room, at the social center of the hotel, makes for a perfect welcome. Rooms range from those in the main lodge to stand-alone chalets and villas with a cozy stone fireplace on one side of the sofa and majestic lake views on the other.

"The chalet-style lodge has one of the most beautiful settings in the country, right on the edge of Queenstown's Lake Wakatipu, with grand views to the aptly named Remarkable Mountains beyond," says Sarah Farag, a director at travel company Southern Crossings. "When guests finally pull themselves away from the view, they'll find the famed Routeburn Track at the doorstep. Everyone loves the rock-star moment when being picked up for the all-but-compulsory helicopter journeys into Fiordland National Park and Milford Sound."

Blanket Bay is 45 minutes from Queenstown; you could combine your time here with a stay at or visit to Rosewood Matakauri (page 383).

OPPOSITE: Blanket Bay offers helicopter tours of nearby Fiordland and Mount Aspiring National Parks.

RM

KANGAROO ISLAND, AUSTRALIA

SOUTHERN OCEAN LODGE

With cliffside ocean views, this rebuilt lodge has survived devastation to come back to life as a leader in luxury and sustainability.

YEAR ESTABLISHED: **2008; reopened 2023** NUMBER OF ROOMS: **25** FAMOUS FEATURE: **Mesmerizing views**
WHEN TO GO: **December–February**

On Kangaroo Island, the second iteration of Southern Ocean Lodge (dubbed SOL 2.0) has opened. In January 2020, as bushfires devastated huge swaths of Australia, the beloved luxury lodge and eco-pioneer since 2008 was completely destroyed, along with around 96 percent of the adjacent national park. The lodge and the ecosystem have been recovering since.

The rebuild of Southern Ocean Lodge—the island's masterpiece of contemporary architecture, with clifftop views and outstanding local food and wine—is a triumphant story after such a significant loss. It's also very personal to owners James and Hayley Baillie, who started Baillie Lodges in 2003 and led the way of new experiential luxury travel in Australia. They now have seven lodges under the collection, including Longitude 131° (page 370) and their flagship, Capella Lodge, on Lord Howe Island.

The Baillies have long been regarded as proactive conservation leaders, and the sustainability of all their lodges is measured on multiple levels. Southern Ocean Lodge has more than 200 solar panels, an innovative wastewater management system, and a goal to be "rainwater self-sufficient."

It's also a dreamy, luxurious, once-in-a-lifetime stay. SOL 2.0 has kept most of the original design footprint but slightly tweaked the suites' locations for even

OPPOSITE: After a long day of exploring Kangaroo Island, rest in the Great Room and soak in the panoramic views of the Southern Ocean.

PAGES 366–367: Southern Ocean Lodge blends seamlessly into the rugged landscape of Kangaroo Island.

better views. The Southern Spa, with Australian-made products, also has a new location.

"I love this lodge for its spectacular location, perched on the cliffs that drop dramatically into the Southern Ocean," says Stuart Rigg, a director of travel company Southern Crossings. "The views are mesmerizing and have always been best enjoyed from the magnificent Great Room."

The center hub of Southern Ocean Lodge, the Great Room features dramatic windows that draw you into the natural world and a serve-yourself bar for anytime drinks and snacks. From here, suites stretch out in a long line, built to blend in with the surrounding landscape. Among the design highlights are artwork from South Australian artists and EcoSmart fireplaces.

Kangaroo Island is the third largest island in Australia and is widely compared to the Galápagos. Just as in the Galápagos, wildlife here roams fearlessly and wildly. Several signature experiences are included in the room rate, including a guided visit to Seal Bay, one of the largest seal colonies in Australia; an outing to see kangaroos and koalas at night; and a half-day guided tour of the national park.

ALTERNATE STAY

To get to Kangaroo Island, it's a short ferry ride or quick flight from Adelaide. Stay a night or two in quaint Adelaide on either end of your trip for upscale beachside dining. Try local favorite Star of Greece. The world-renowned Barossa Valley wine region is less than an hour northeast of the city.

SYDNEY, AUSTRALIA

PARK HYATT SYDNEY

With views of the Sydney Opera House outside your window, this standout hotel opens the door to explore Australia's best known city.

YEAR ESTABLISHED: 1990 **NUMBER OF ROOMS: 155** **FAMOUS FEATURE: Sydney Opera House views**
WHEN TO GO: Year-round

A stay at the harborfront Park Hyatt Sydney is an indulgent way to see the city. The hotel's icon status is intertwined with its awe-inspiring views of the world-famous architectural masterpiece Sydney Opera House, which opened in 1959. The opera house is a traveler's first introduction to the famous city and a gateway to exploring its diverse dining, vibrant neighborhoods, and myriad museums and outdoor pursuits, including the stunning 3.5-mile (5.6 km) Bondi Beach walking path to the beachfront suburb of Coogee.

"This is *the* place to enjoy postcard views across the harbor to the Sydney Opera House, but beyond that, the hotel offers a level of sophistication and service that makes visitors feel instantly at home and infinitely indulged," says Stuart Rigg, a director at travel company Southern Crossings. "The hotel's ultraluxe Sydney Suite has an incredible outdoor terrace with panoramic views."

Close by is the start of the BridgeClimb, a chance to ascend the Sydney Harbour Bridge. It's not for those scared of heights, but a hugely rewarding experience for those that give it a go. This is a flagship for the Hyatt brand (Palacio Duhau - Park Hyatt Buenos Aires, see page 266, is another standout), so Hyatt loyalty points will go far here.

ALTERNATE STAY

Combine a visit to bustling Sydney with one to more laid-back, breezy Melbourne. Two hours away on Phillip Island, thousands of penguins emerge from the ocean each evening in what is known as the Penguin Parade. Or check in to Glen Isla House (see page 378), an absolutely charming B&B offering fantastic homemade breakfasts.

OPPOSITE: This deluxe room with a king bed at the Park Hyatt offers a view of the famous Sydney Opera House.

NORTHERN TERRITORY, AUSTRALIA

LONGITUDE 131°

Keep your eye on the mythical red rocks while watching the sun rise at this luxurious tented camp.

YEAR ESTABLISHED: 2002 **NUMBER OF ROOMS:** 16 **FAMOUS FEATURE:** Sunrise on the red rocks
WHEN TO GO: May–September

The Australian outback is vast and sparsely populated for a reason—it's tough living, with few natural resources. But deep in the outback, nestled in the magical red rocks of Uluṟu-Kata Tjuṯa National Park in Australia's Northern Territory, is the desert-luxe retreat Longitude 131°. With just 16 white tents, all with views of the mythical rock formations—both Uluṟu and Kata Tjuṯa—the lodge's terraces make for perfect spots to watch the sun light up the red rocks as it rises.

"While I love the romance of the canopied pavilions and waking up to views of Uluṟu, the standout feature of Longitude 131° has to be sleeping under the outback stars," says Stuart Rigg, a director at travel company Southern Crossings. "Every guest tent has an outdoor private deck which can be set up to enjoy spectacular stargazing with turndown service and a fireplace at your feet."

Like all Baillie Lodges (see Southern Ocean Lodge, page 364), sustainability is at the core of the property, which operates with minimal impact to protect the area and even leave it better. Part of this mission is preserving cultural heritage, which guests can do through included signature experiences such as guided hikes to learn about Aboriginal culture or simply visiting Uluṟu at sunset, offered with a private pop-up bar.

The resort's heart is the Dune House, where all meals are served. It has a library for those who wish to learn more about the area's history, too. The spa uses local products such as Australian clay in its treatments, the perfect way to cap a day of desert exploration.

OPPOSITE: **The distant Uluṟu, Australia's famous sandstone formation, rises over Longitude 131°'s many luxurious dwellings.**

TASMANIA, AUSTRALIA

SAFFIRE FREYCINET

With a special aim to protect and grow the Tasmanian devil population, this noteworthy hotel offers a rare look into the natural world.

YEAR ESTABLISHED: **2010** NUMBER OF ROOMS: **20** FAMOUS FEATURE: **Tasmanian devils**
WHEN TO GO: **December–February**

Saffire Freycinet is set in an otherworldly corner of the island of Tasmania (or Tassie, for Australians), with views to the distinctly shaped Hazards mountains and curving sapphire-colored Oyster Bay, where dolphins frolic and local farmers harvest oysters for the hotel's ever changing menu. Surrounding the property is lush Freycinet National Park, a coastal rainforest that includes nearby Wineglass Bay (what a name!) and wombat sightings.

Part of Saffire Freycinet's mission is to protect Tasmanian devils. The hotel is a sponsor of the Tasmanian government's Save the Tasmanian Devil Program. Aside from cartoons and memes, few know what a Tassie devil actually is, so let us explain: The world's largest remaining carnivorous marsupial is now also an endangered species. The population has dropped significantly since the 1990s, when a rare, quick-spreading cancer devastated the devils. The hotel operates what they call a "luxury retirement home" on-site for devils who have produced offspring, and guests can visit and learn about the efforts to save them.

The design feels like a mix of Scandi meets Northern California, a sophisticated lodge with clean lines and cozy light wood, all with windows framing views to the natural world.

QUOTABLE

"This is one of my favorite Australian luxury lodges," says Stuart Rigg, a director at Southern Crossings. "There is an exceptional level of relaxed and friendly service—and the lodge's delicious dining experiences showcase the very finest Tasmanian produce."

OPPOSITE: The Saffire Freycinet lounge offers spectacular views of the Hazards mountains and surrounding Freycinet National Park.

TETIAROA ISLAND, FRENCH POLYNESIA

THE BRANDO

Sustainability doesn't mean sacrifice on this private island retreat where luxury comes before all else.

YEAR ESTABLISHED: **2014** NUMBER OF ROOMS: **35** FAMOUS FEATURE: **Seawater-powered air-conditioning**
WHEN TO GO: **May–October**

Few people realize that actor Marlon Brando—a Hollywood icon with a turbulent personal history—was a staunch environmentalist. After filming *Mutiny on the Bounty* in the 1960s, Brando fell in love with French Polynesia and bought Tetiaroa Island, a private atoll 30 miles (48 km) from Tahiti, once the exclusive retreat of Tahitian kings. The annular reef around the island has no navigable path; kings would cross in outrigger canoes. Today, nearly everyone arrives via twin-turboprop airplane on twice-daily 15-minute flights from Tahiti's international airport.

Brando spent decades living in relative isolation on the island before approaching longtime hotel developer Dick Bailey, chairman of Pacific Beachcomber and an American who had lived in Tahiti since 1986, about opening a resort. Although Brando died 10 years before the hotel opened in 2014, the two developed a more enriching visitor experience that aimed to leave the island in better condition than they'd found it.

The result is not only one of the dreamiest hotel experiences in the world, but also a property that takes sustainability to a remarkable level through technological innovation and a close partnership with the Tetiaroa Society. "Our tourism model is doing well by doing right," says Bailey.

Visitors come from all over the world to see how one of the most pioneering technologies works. Originally Brando's idea, the resort's air-conditioning is entirely cooled by seawater. "We put a pipe down right off the reef, a 3,000-foot [914 m] drop near the bottom of the ocean where the water is very, very cold," says Bailey. "The water comes up to the surface by hydrostatic

ALTERNATE STAY

"The sustainability model applies even if you're not a luxury property," says Bailey. "Three of our properties are in the three-star category." Check out other Pacific Beachcomber properties in French Polynesia, including the InterContinental Tahiti, where many spend the night before continuing on to The Brando.

OPPOSITE: **Tumi Brando, granddaughter of Marlon Brando, swims through a coral garden.**

pressure, like a straw in a glass. We don't use energy to draw it up but capture the cold and use it to air-condition the entire property, including our staff housing." The remaining 25 percent of energy needed comes from more than 4,000 solar panels and burning coconut oil. Mosquitoes on the island are nearly eradicated, thanks to an innovative program that sterilizes larva and stops reproduction. "My hope is that The Brando comes to stand for a certain type of [sustainable] tourism, not just one property," says Bailey.

With no light pollution in French Polynesia, you may—in many ways—feel like you've not truly seen the sky before you looked up here. It's also simply one of the most luxe, relaxing holidays you'll ever have. We're talking private villas; diving, snorkeling, and swimming; a fitness center and tennis courts; and delicious food featuring fresh produce such as papayas, limes, bananas, vanilla, and honey all harvested on the atoll.

ABOVE: **Children and parents alike will appreciate a bike ride around Onetahi.**

OPPOSITE: **A stunning sunset view of the South Pacific Ocean from a villa at The Brando**

OCEANIA

BONUS STAYS

AUSTRALIA

COMO The Treasury, *Perth*

Locals joke that Perth is as far away as you can get. If you've made your way to this part of Western Australia, you want to base yourself at its historic center. The 48-room COMO is housed in a 19th-century structure within the revitalized State Buildings. It's surrounded by shops, restaurants, and galleries. Within the hotel is one of the COMO brand specialties, an excellent Shambhala spa. Fun fact: This is geographical point zero for Perth, from which all other points are measured.

Glen Isla House, *Phillip Island*

Phillip Island is known for the evening Penguin Parade, when thousands of the adorable creatures waddle on the beach from the ocean (there's a viewing platform to enjoy the nightly show). Stay at Glen Isla House, an absolutely charming B&B—with equally lovely owners and one of the best homemade breakfasts.

Jackalope Mornington Peninsula, *Merricks North*

Though the Mornington Peninsula isn't as well known as the Yarra Valley, both are easily accessible to Melbourne—and have their own charms. The Jackalope opened in 2017 on its own vineyard, and the style (with lots of black and gold) is urban chic meets Australian farm. It's a nice stopping point between visits to Melbourne and Phillip Island.

Kittawa Lodge, *Tasmania*

Located on what is considered one of Australia's best kept secrets, King Island, Kittawa Lodge feels gloriously remote, though there are direct flights from Melbourne. Two one-bedroom lodges are both set on a stretch of beautiful coastline. The owners, Aaron Suine and Nick Stead, wanted to create a special retreat for sophisticated travelers, but also a slower-paced life for themselves. Dream achieved.

Lizard Island, *Lizard Island*

This is the place to experience the Great Barrier Reef in style. Lizard Island is remote and exclusive, a one-hour charter flight from Cairns. "You can step straight off the beach to snorkel over Technicolor corals and clam gardens, swim with turtles, and enjoy access to some of the world's best dive sites," says Stuart Rigg, a director at Southern Crossings. Tour the Lizard Island Research Station, operated by the Australian Museum, for real insight on the reef and its conservation.

OPPOSITE: Take an excursion to the outer area of the Great Barrier Reef during your stay at Lizard Island.

PAGES 380–381: Vacation at New Zealand's Huka Lodge, where you'll enjoy indoor and outdoor spaces that seamlessly blend together.

NEW ZEALAND
THE COUNTRY FOR THE
ANGLER

The Louise, *Marananga*
The perfect base to explore the winelands of the Barossa Valley near Adelaide, The Louise has 15 elegant private suites to choose from. Among the other offerings: a vineyard-facing infinity pool, a light-filled dining room that is a destination on its own, and bookable experiences, such as a picnic breakfast enjoyed while getting close to local kangaroos.

NEW ZEALAND

Acacia Cliffs Lodge, *Taupō*
In the center of the North Island and set on a ridge overlooking the largest lake in New Zealand, this beautifully designed lodge has four luxurious rooms (three with lake views and one facing the garden) and common areas with floor-to-ceiling windows. The standout hosts are gracious and kind. Don't miss walking down to Acacia Bay for a swim.

Huka Lodge, *Taupō*
Known as the original luxury fly-fishing lodge of New Zealand, Huka Lodge was first established in 1924 on the banks of the Waikato River on the North Island. Later it became a favorite of Queen Elizabeth II. Today, the lodge offers a range of adventure offerings and locally sourced dining—from the salad leaves and tomatoes to the chicken, meat, and fish options.

Minaret Station, *Wānaka*
Located close to Queenstown and accessible only by helicopter, family-owned

ABOVE: In Tasmania, Kittawa Lodge serves a delicious charcuterie board of cheese, pickles, meat, and olives.

OPPOSITE: A family watches a herd of sheep during a farm tour at Rosewood Kauri Cliffs, which is part of New Zealand's Robertson Lodges.

Minaret Station is set in a glacial valley, a prime jumping-off point for all New Zealand adventure itineraries. The hotel offers an incredible dining program; all food is sourced from their own private farm. There are just four private chalets, making it one of the most exclusive luxury experiences in the world.

Pihopa Retreat, *Nelson*
With just six suites, this inviting retreat on the South Island is located near the creative hub of Nelson, on the grounds of a former bishop's residence. Within a short drive are beautiful beaches, craft breweries, vineyards, cycling trails, and national parks, including Abel Tasman.

Robertson Lodges, *various locations*
These three ultraluxe lodges, now managed by Rosewood Hotels, started as the passion project of entrepreneur Julian Robertson, which his family continued after his passing. Rosewood Kauri Cliffs and Rosewood Cape Kidnappers are two of the world's great golf and leisure resorts; Rosewood Matakauri is close to Queenstown, set directly on Lake Wakatipu and surrounded by mountains.

HOW TO BE A BETTER GUEST

The Four Seasons Hotels started in Toronto in 1961 and have become synonymous with ultraluxe properties, but as founder Isadore Sharp says: "The reason for our success is no secret. It comes down to one single principle that transcends time and geography, religion, and culture. It's the Golden Rule—the simple idea that if you treat people well, the way you would like to be treated, they will do the same."

In hospitality, this rule is not one-sided. As guests and travelers, we must treat everyone the way we want to be treated, no matter their job title.

What follows are some tips to be a considerate guest during your stay:

To be a good guest, try being a good host.

As Dick Bailey, owner of The Brando, says, "To be a good guest, try being a good host." Try throwing a couple dinner parties before a hotel stay. As the host, you can find simple fixes for most dinner party failures: The chicken is raw? Order pizza, no problem. It mostly comes down to being an affable, solution-oriented host able to roll with the inevitable complications that arise. The idea here: Whether invited guests or hotel guests, don't overreact to bumpy situations. The best hotel managers exude this adaptable attitude, and the best hotel guests recognize that everyone is doing the best they can.

In public spaces, it is your duty to switch on.

When you arrive at a hotel lobby, to airport security, or to a taxi queue, valet parking, or anywhere that requires interacting with other human beings, you have a duty to switch on. Remove your headphones, look up from your phone (or better yet, put it away), and pay attention. Yes, this means exiting your

OPPOSITE: A courteous porter opens a door to welcome guests.

private, personal bubble, but everyone deserves that decency. Bonus points for a smile and a sense of humor.

Seek out alternative places and times.

Many of us are familiar with the term "overtourism," referencing the warring crowds that battle it out on any given day during summer in Italy, for instance, or New York City before Christmas. To help alleviate the stress, travelers are leaning into "microtourism"—travel that's just an hour or two away from home—but that has its own challenges depending on where you live (think about the Louvre in Paris or the British Museum in London during school breaks). Considering both trends, it's easier to play a part in the solution: Seek out alternative places and alternative times to visit, if possible. Among ideas for Europe: Try any museum in Rome in January; visit London neighborhoods outside zone 1 on the Tube; or hike in the stunning Slovenian Alps instead of the Dolomites.

Stay curious.

Travelers who have a wide variety of interests and care deeply about learning—whether about history and museums, fashion and shopping, food and wine, or hiking and wellness—are more likely to seek out responsible travel experiences. Part of being a better guest is also seeking out quality licensed and/or professionally trained guides who are trusted and make a career out of showcasing a destination. Blue Badge guides in the United Kingdom, for instance, study for 18 months to two years before they qualify to lead tours.

Respect the dress code.

Some hotels still have dress codes, whether to continue long-held traditions or ensure the glamour of a dining experience. Fashion is, to say the least, constantly evolving. Today, jeans and a blouse or blazer are stylish and appropriate for most occasions, personalized to you. But it's important you acknowledge the expectations of a hotel. You should feel welcome and kindly treated no matter what you're wearing—and we've all arrived bleary-eyed from an overnight flight—but what you wear should reflect the tone of your trip.

OPPOSITE: **A golden-hued hotel room key**

DESTINATIONS BY LOCATION

ACKNOWLEDGMENTS

This book is a dream come true, the culmination of a 20-plus-year career based on a love for many aspects of this business. I have relied on the support and kindness of so many people.

To editorial director at National Geographic Books, Lisa Thomas, for listening to my pitch (again) and connecting me to my wonderful editor, Allyson Johnson. Allyson—thank you for letting me be me. You have an extraordinary gift. Keith Bellows gave me a shot at National Geographic when we created my role as Urban Insider. I always miss him. To my original Nat Geo crew, especially Kim Connaghan, Heather Wyatt, John Campbell, and Andrew Nelson (the ultimate wordsmith).

Also thank you to designer Kay Hankins and photo editor Susan Blair for bringing these hotels to life on these pages, and to Becca Saltzman for seeing it through the finish line.

To those who embody hospitality for me and many others: Valentina De Santis, Marco Novella, Ori Kafri, Ben Trodd, Niall Rochford, Paula Carroll, Riccardo Ortogni, Samuel Leizorek, Markos Chaidemenos, Paula Fitzherbert, Claudio Meli, Matthias Kaesweber, Anna Roost, and Urs Langenegger.

To these travel industry titans for their passion, insight, and friendship while writing this: the incomparable Jack Ezon at Embark Beyond, Mattej Valenčič, Matej Knific, Andrea Grisdale (queen), Maita Barrenechea, Will Kiburz, Stuart Rigg, Sonia Graupera, Zach Rabinor, Gilad Berenstein, Ricarda Lindner, Jules Maury, J.MAK, Carrie Culpepper, Simon Leadsford, Limor Decter, Matt Biden, Jo Bailes, Shannon Knapp, Kristien Deleersnijder, Carolina Perez, Anthony Goldman, Chadner Navarro. Matthew Upchurch at Virtuoso for being a visionary, always. Melissa Biggs Bradley, Eliza Scott Harris, and Simone Girner at Indagare.

Jules Perowne for your boundless generosity and support. PR royalty: Laura Davidson, Alice Marshall, Sarah Evans, Lucy Clifton, Gabriele Sappok, Kristen Vigrass, James Treacy, Melanie Brandman, Lee Edelstein, and Team Geoffrey Weill: Ann Laschever and Mark Liebermann.

To dear friends I was lucky to meet in this industry: Ellen Asmodeo-Giglio (a true powerhouse), Susan Zurbin-Hothersall, and James Shillinglaw. Divia Thani for your thought leadership and kindness, no matter how big your title.

Kevin O'Leary and Samantha Brown, for showing us the way with heart and a lot of humor. We miss being near you in Brooklyn. I am so honored your words open this book, Sam. Misty Belles, my vault, whose friendship transcends the industry. Becca Hensley, my wonderful friend and all-time favorite writer. Lauren Bryan Knight, for loving Nancy Myers and friendships made in pretty places as much as I do.

Friends old and new: Caroline Moats Geer, Emma de Vadder, Jerramy Fine, Sian Parry, Kirsten Magen, Whitney Haldeman, Michael Carroll, Dana Zukofsky, Devon Fredericks, Johanne Killeen, Sheyi Martins-Allen, Liz Taylor, Adrienne Barber, Ashley Pittman, Michaela Ruoss, Stephanie Steinman, Amber Mickelson, Julia Langdal, John O'Ceallaigh, Barbara Sackheim King, Lish Steiling, Abbey Cook, Julie Morgan, Elizabeth Essex, Laura McMurchie, Shannon Rice, Emily Wright, and Dayna Brandoff. Whitney Wolfe Herd for taking the power of one connection global. Andy Ellwood for the original Hotel Belle sweatshirt and *The Alchemist*. Nevin Dereköy and Ashleigh Bunten—thank you.

Being one of five kids informs every aspect of your life (including wanting your own hotel room). For this, I am forever grateful. Thank you, Greg, Tim, Michael, and Maggie (Bit); Tom and Teresa Fitzsimmons; and beyond—Merilee, Idamae, Emmilou; Christina Riggio and Charlie Jackson (buffer). I have an amazing extended family, including Carol Pontrelli, Erin Buckley, Kate Schwartz, the Herrmann family, and Max Rzehulka.

I am equally a homebody (with a massive cookbook collection) and world traveler; I love coming home. Alex Herrmann, Dapper: for your equal partnership and the serendipity of #7020. Sophie Lyons Herrmann: my greatest gift. I love you more than anything, even the Cipriani in Venice.

For every person who works in hotels—you create magic in people's lives, the power of which cannot be underestimated. A career in this industry is so much more than a job. And I know it can be exhausting. Thank you.

ILLUSTRATIONS CREDITS

Cover, Grand Hotel Tremezzo; back cover, Dook; 2-3, Six Senses Bhutan; 4-5, Great Plains; 7, Baros Maldives; 8, Sirikoi Lodge; 9, Ydo Sol; 11, Sim Canetty Clarke; 12-3, Schloss Elmau; 14, Relais Christine and @MisterTripper; 15, Auberge Resorts Collection; 16, Adare Manor; 19-21, Belmond Images; 23-26, Grand Hotel Tremezzo; 27, Fondazione Gualtiero Marchesi (Gualtiero Marchesi Foundation); 29, Claudio Beduschi/REDA&CO/Universal Images Group via Getty Images; 31-3, Umberto D'Aniello; 35, Borgo San Felice; 37, Dario Garofalo; 39, courtesy of Hotel de Russie; 41, Elizabeth Minchilli; 42-3, Serenity-H/Shutterstock; 45-53, Red Carnation Hotels; 55-9, Claridge's; 61-5, THE PIG Hotel Group/Jake Eastham; 67-9, Sim Canetty Clarke; 71, Frank Fell/robertharding; 73, MarøyKlouda-221; 74-5, 62°NORD/Christian Remøy; 76-7, 62°NORD; 79-81, Magnus Mårding; 83, courtesy of d'Angleterre; 85, Dominik Baumgartner; 87, Tschuggen Collection, Hotel Eden Roc; 89, gorillaimages/Shutterstock; 90-1, Ydo Sol; 93, The Living Circle/Tom Egli; 95, @MisterTripper; 96-7, Relais Christine and @MisterTripper; 99, Emmanuelle Marty; 100-1, Martino Dini; 103, Massimo Listri; 105, The Maybourne Riviera; 107, Eric Gaillard/Reuters/Redux; 109, © Bernard Winkelmann; 110-1, © Richard Haughton; 113, The Fontenay Hamburg; 115, Schloss Elmau/Fridolin Full; 116-7, Schloss Elmau/Andreas Vallbracht; 118, Schloss Elmau/Fridolin Full; 119, Schloss Elmau/Kriner-Weiermann; 121, Hotel am Steinplatz, Autograph Collection; 123-5, © Sacher Hotels; 127, Ronald Tilleman; 129-131, Hospitality Builders; 133, Adolfo Rancaño; 135, courtesy Four Seasons Hotel Ritz Lisbon; 137, courtesy Hotel Grande Bretagne; 139, fokke baarssen/Shutterstock; 140-1, Yiorgos Kordakis; 143, Riccardo Lavezzo in Fiorenzo Calosso, Castle Otočec; 144, Saša Hess, Castle Otočec; 145, Riccardo Lavezzo in Fiorenzo Calosso, Castle Otočec; 147, © Kempinski Hotels; 149, Guadalupe Laiz; 151, Borgo Engazia; 152-3, Asim Ali Malik/Shutterstock; 154, Guido Fuà - Eikona Studio; 155, courtesy Finca Cortesin; 156-7, courtesy Grand Hotel Majestic "già Baglioni"; 158-163, Kodiak Greenwood/Post Ranch Inn; 165, The Beverly Hills Hotel, Dorchester Collection; 167, Michael Orso/Getty Images; 169, Simon Brown Photography, Crosby Street Hotel, Firmdale Hotels; 170-1, Quentin Bacon, Crosby Street Hotel, Firmdale Hotels; 173, Four Seasons Resort Maui; 174-5, Four Seasons Resort Hualalai; 176, Robb Gordon; 177, Four Seasons Resort Oahu at Ko Olina; 179, The Walt Disney Company/Kent Phillips; 180-1, The Walt Disney Company/Dan Forer; 183, Brush Creek Ranch; 185, The Hay-Adams; 187-9, Auberge Resorts Collection; 191-3, The Hermosa Inn; 195-7, Castle Hot

Springs; 199, Inn of the Five Graces; 201, Blackberry Mountain/Ingalls Photography; 202, Blackberry Farm/Jessica Grant; 203, Blackberry Mountain/Ingalls Photography; 205, Montage Palmetto Bluff; 207, Uzzell Lambert/courtesy of Kiawah Island Golf Resort; 209, courtesy of Connie Zhou; 210-1, Diana Todorova Photography; 213, Eric Martin/Figarophoto/Redux; 215, Hector Velasco for Las Alcobas Mexico City; 217-9, Tanveer Badal; 221, Jean-Philippe Piter, Eden Rock - St Barths; 223, Eric Rubens for Belmond; 224-5, Cap Juluca, A Belmond Hotel, Anguilla; 227, sep120/Stockimo/Alamy Stock Photo; 228-9, Mircea Costina/Alamy Stock Photo; 231-3, Alex Fradkin; 235, courtesy Hacienda de San Antonio, photography by Davis Gerber; 236-7, courtesy of COMO Parrot Cay; 238, Jason Risner; 239, Vanessa Leroy/The New York Times/Redux; 240-1, Carrie Cole Photography/Getty Images; 242-3, Federico García/Awasi Patagonia; 245, Wilbert Das/UXUA; 247-251, Vik Retreats; 253, Carolina Vargas; 255-7, Luciano Bacchi/Awasi Patagonia; 259, Tom Escobar; 261, Javier Falcón for Belmond; 262, powerofforever/Getty Images; 263, Adrian Huston for Belmond; 265, courtesy of Nayara Springs; 267, Palacio Duhau – Park Hyatt Buenos Aires; 268-9, Casa de Uco Vineyards & Wine Resort; 270, courtesy The Vines; 271, Luis War/Shutterstock; 272-3, Umaid Bhawan Palace, Jodhpur; 275, Sebastian Suki Belaustegui; 276-7, Tania Araujo; 279, Ori Ackermann; 281, Ralf Tooten/laif/Redux; 283, courtesy of Hoshino Resorts; 285, courtesy of Hiiragiya Ryokan; 287-9, Mandarin Oriental; 291, Oberoi Hotels & Resorts; 293, Umaid Bhawan Palace, Jodhpur; 295, The Peninsula Hong Kong; 297, Waldorf Astoria Shanghai on the Bund; 299-301, Six Senses Bhutan; 303, Baros Maldives; 305-7, Oberoi Hotels & Resorts; 308, Lesterman/Shutterstock; 309, The Reverie Saigon; 310-1, Dook for Angama; 313-5, courtesy of La Mamounia; 317, Marc Dozier/hemis/Alamy Stock Photo; 318-320, Ahmet Gül; 321, hemro/Shutterstock; 323, Sammy Njoroge for Angama; 325-7, Sirikoi Lodge; 329, Singita; 330, Captured at Singita, Ross Couper; 331-3, Singita; 335-7, The Royal Portfolio; 339, Dook/Tswalu; 341: Mwiba Lodge, Legendary Expeditions, Tanzania; 343, courtesy Londolozi Game Reserve; 345-7, Wilderness; 349, Great Plains; 351, Sonja Kilian; 352-3, Dook; 354, Miavana by Time + Tide; 355, Dar Ahlam; 356-9, courtesy Wharekauhau; 361, Otahuna Lodge; 363, Alpine Heli Blanket Bay; 365-7, George Apostolidis; 369, David Mitchener; 371, George Apostolidis; 373, Saffire Freycinet; 375, Eric Martin/Figarophoto/Redux; 376, The Brando - Barry Grossman; 377, The Brando - World Stompers; 379, Alex Kydd; 380-1, Richard Brimer; 382, Rosewood Kauri Cliffs; 383, Wilderness Weddings; 384, Nick Dolding/Getty Images; 386, Tetra Images/Getty Images.

ABOUT THE AUTHOR

Annie Fitzsimmons has covered hotels, travel, lifestyle, restaurants, and destinations around the world for the last two decades across many platforms and in a constantly evolving media landscape. She has worked with top media and travel brands, including at Indagare as editorial director, AFAR Media, and Virtuoso. She held various roles over the course of almost a decade at National Geographic Travel, including luxury editor, editor at large, and the first and only Urban Insider, reporting on cities, culture, and people around the world. So far, she has hosted more than 40 trips across Europe for small and large groups, planned itineraries for private clients, and created hundreds of travel guides. Fitzsimmons has been a keynote speaker and panelist about trends and luxury travel at conferences and events around the world and a host for podcasts, online series, and shows. From Scottsdale, Arizona, she lived in New York City for 10 years and has been a licensed New York City tour guide since 2008. Currently based in London with her family, Fitzsimmons has traveled to six continents for work and will make it to Antarctica one day.

Since 1888, the National Geographic Society has funded more than 14,000 research, conservation, education, and storytelling projects around the world. National Geographic Partners distributes a portion of the funds it receives from your purchase to National Geographic Society to support programs including the conservation of animals and their habitats.

National Geographic Partners, LLC
1145 17th Street NW
Washington, DC 20036-4688 USA

Get closer to National Geographic Explorers and photographers, and connect with our global community. Join us today at nationalgeographic.org/joinus

For rights or permissions inquiries, please contact National Geographic Books Subsidiary Rights: bookrights@natgeo.com

ISBN: 978-1-4262-2315-0

Printed in South Korea

24/QPSK/1

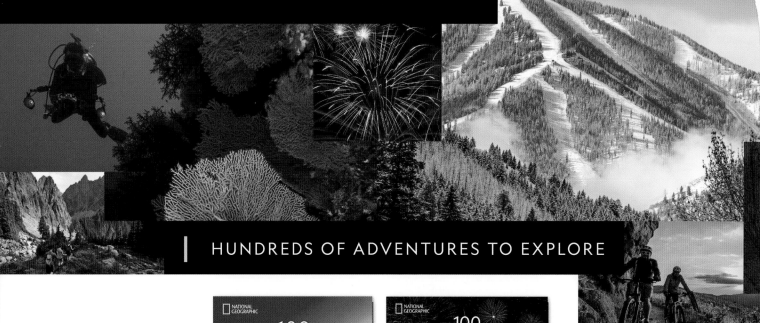

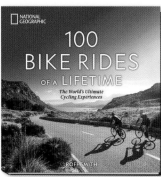

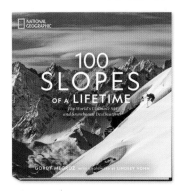

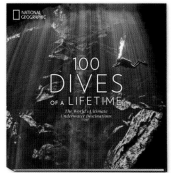